To The
Beautiful

M000234778

Epistles to Abba

You are such
a tremendous blessing
your smile & grace
can lighten any room
Thank you for all your
assistance always

DR. M Caulli

07.2021

Epistles to Abba

Letters from the Heart

DR. SOPHIA MATTIS

I AM Ignites

New York

Epistles to Abba: Letters from the Heart by Dr. Sophia Mattis

Published by I Am Ignites
209 Glen Cove Rd. Suite 508
Carle Place, NY 11514

The author has made every attempt to note accurate Internet addresses during the time of publication, neither the author nor publisher assume any liability for errors or changes occurring after the publication of the book.

ISBN: 978-1-7344795-1-5

Library of Congress Control Number: 2020912656

Printed in the United States of America.

Cover design by Ruben Arana & Dr. Sophia Mattis

Acknowledgments

I dedicate this book to Abba, my Father – GOD Almighty who was, who *is* and who will *always* be my greatest source of inspiration. To my LORD and Savior Jesus Christ of Nazareth who has given me the greatest gift in life – eternal salvation! And last but definitely not least, to the Holy Spirit who continually rekindles my fire. Blessed be GOD, who blesses us abundantly!

Unmeasurable love to my parents Errol & Winniefred Mattis. Mom and dad, a tremendous thank you for the many years of continued support and unrestrained love.

Thank you to *all* my Christian brothers and sisters and my non-Christian friends alike for always supporting the mission of Jesus Christ of Nazareth.

My Love,

I love you darling, but you don't know that yet. Stella, Rosa, Hazel Crest? Let's paint that sunshine red! What's that you say? I'm as tough as those pretty little

peach artisan nails. Now, let's see, California surfing, hum, some nursing I'll need. Ambergris Caye here we come. We plan on experiencing that very blue sea, royal blue hole is all I need. Ambergris, so very sorry to say, although you're magnificently serene, hubby and I won't be on our way. See you after we visit the tropics in Jamaica West Indies. So here I go, no wait, there we go, off to the city with the sea, in that very place where he watches me! And finally, to Anaranebur my dream catcher who snatches my very concepts and thoughts to brings them to life.

Forever my love,

Lady in Red

Preface

Here's my confession, I'm nervous! The uniqueness of this book has me a bit anxious. I'll admit, it's the sort of nervousness that comes about when the unknown presents itself. This is not the typical book of prayers. The style, the order, the rhetoric, they all present in what some may say is an odd sort of way and maybe even unacceptable language or address. This includes even the table of contents which only list the numbered epistle without naming the person who is praying. This was intentionally done as a way to maintain the element of surprise for the reader. I thank GOD with every fiber of my being, He helps me trust Him.

By no means is this book inclusive of every situation imaginable. A demonstration of *all* situations is an impossible feat. The compilation of prayers in this book was inspired by the Spirit of the Lord. It was GOD Almighty who impressed each scenario in my heart. He whispered to my soul the very thoughts of others while instructing me to share those thoughts with the world.

Epistles to Abba: Letters from the Heart was written to bring healing, hope, rest, and restoration to countless people. This book serves to incite a deeper sense of compassion within those who never expressed severe trauma or hurt and to help those who've been severely hurt by resurrecting and reuniting them with the innocence of love they once had.

Epistles to Abba: Letters from the Heart is a book intended to help its readers fully understand the essence of prayer. This book is intended to help each reader realize that prayer is not regimented, restricted nor restrictive, and that prayer is merely one having a conversation with GOD. I'm confident in saying, I know many will profit from the contents within this book. The 53 Epistles, a.k.a. letters, stem from the views of its petitioner, based on their current situation.

Presently, to my knowledge, there are no other books of this kind. Again, this *is* a book of prayers, but not your typical book of prayers. In a traditional book of prayers, the author reveals prayers intended to guide the reader through how to pray by providing an instructional format or semi-tutorial layout. Authors of traditional prayer books generally provide prayers that revere GOD, a manner most Christians would consider acceptable. However, in *Epistles to Abba: Letters from the Heart*, the reader will quickly realize there's no template or formulary of reverential prayers. Each prayer is offered to GOD from the prayer's situational vantage point. I suppose one may even go as far as calling this an *unorthodox* approach to the "acceptable" prayer.

Introduction

"The thief does not come except to steal, and to kill, and to destroy. I have come that they may have life, and that they may have it more abundantly." ~ <u>John 10 10</u> (NKJV)

Blessed be our GOD who blesses us abundantly!

I began writing short stories in the 4th grade. I started writing everything Christian when I started hearing the voice of the LORD. His voice was as clear as 2 people having a conversation at the dinner table. The Father began sharing various things with me about why people said and did certain things. He'd reveal to me, the true heart of many people. For example, a person would either say to me or I'd hear them say to someone, "I'm not going tonight. I'm pretty tired, so I'm just going to stay home." While everyone was busy believing what they just said, in the interim, I'd hear the Father say, "They don't have the money to go to the event."

As a child, I never felt as if GOD didn't hear me when I spoke. I'm not even sure I did the "expected" form of prayer. I used to talk to GOD knowing without a shadow of a doubt, He was listening. Oddly enough, as I've matured, I sometimes find myself wondering if GOD is listening to my prayers. Thankfully, I catch myself pretty quickly and nip that thought in the bud. I know GOD is always listening. For GOD is not a man that He should lie nor the son of man that He shall repent. GOD said He would never leave us nor forsake us. It is in those truths I gain my resolute conviction. *"God is not a man, that he should lie; neither the son of man, that he should repent: hath he said, and shall he not do it? or hath he spoken, and shall he not make it good?"*~ <u>Numbers 23:19</u>. *"Let your conversation be without covetousness; and be content with such things as ye have: for he hath said, I will never leave thee, nor forsake thee."*~ <u>Hebrews 13:5</u>. Amid both extremes, I recall times of exploration where I'd pray: at specific times, lit a candle, wore head-coverings, prayed both out loud and in silence, spoke eloquently and quite frankly, sometimes just simplistically. There were times I focused solely on praying spiritual warfare prayers and times when my prayers encompassed no spiritual warfare at all. Sometimes my prayers were scripture laden, while other times I used not one scripture. The truth is, my pray life has run the gamut! I'm delighted to say, with the Father's help, I am no longer behaving like a pendulum, wavering in my thoughts on the correct way to communicate with GOD. I thank GOD He's taught me in the school of the Holy Ghost how to simply just talk to Him. I thank GOD He made it clear to me that He knows *all* our thoughts before we even have them.

In *Epistles to Abba: Letters from the Heart*, every epistle/letter was directly downloaded into my spirit from the Holy Spirit. Surprisingly, it was in 2010 that GOD revealed to me the sorts of prayers offered to Him. Fast-forward 10 years later in 2020, I heard the Father say, "It's time to release *this* book." He then said, "Many people are questioning how to pray, thinking their prayers are ineffective or not being heard at all. It's good this book follows *Christianity 101: The ABC's and 123's of The Faith* because they would've read the chapter on prayer and praying. Now that they've read the basics of Christianity, the next step is to assure they understand and are comfortable with the essence of prayer. This is the time to teach and reassure people never to break the line of communication with Me by not praying because of feelings of inadequacy or uncertainty."

This book was written to help abolish the very notion some hold regarding how one *ought* to pray or how they *should* communicate with GOD. Beloved, many have heard others refer to a god, but the fact is, some persons have never been taught about the *true* and living GOD. As such, one's first recognizable encounter with the Father by way of prayer may demonstrate an unintentional lack of respect.

In this book, you'll encounter some prayers containing misquoted scripture(s). This was purposefully done to depict an individual who is incorrectly diving the Word of GOD. Meaning, the petitioner has not studied to show himself approved. [15]*"Study to shew thyself approved unto God, a workman that needeth not to be ashamed, rightly dividing the word of truth."* ~ 2 Timothy 2:15

During your reading, you may find some of the prayers quite humorous while others you may find offensive although it is not my intension to offend you. Keep in mind that all the prayers in this book are examples of real prayers offered to the Father. My beloved readers, GOD *does* have a sense of humor and so should you! Additionally, you'll encounter fictitious words intentionally written, to signify a child's underdeveloped language. Let me reiterate, these prayers are not ones I've said to the Father, they are prayers I've obtained from the Holy Spirit. *[13] "Then were there brought unto him little children, that he should put his hands on them, and pray: and the disciples rebuked them. [14] But Jesus said, Suffer little children, and forbid them not, to come unto me: for of such is the kingdom of heaven." ~* <u>Matthew 19:13-14</u>.

The core of this book is found in the section titled, *The Epistles* where you will find a unique compilation of individualized prayers promising to captivate your attention. With a melodramatic style, the prayers displayed in this book are sure to remain in your spirit, reminding you that your prayers should be unrestrained conversations with GOD. The theme of each epistle pivots around this elemental ideology: irrespective of one's age, religious affiliation, gender, race, or circumstance, GOD hears and listens to *all* prayers.

Many Letters from the Heart

In the face of trials and tribulations, it's almost inevitable that feelings of isolation may plague you. Such feelings are inevitable. You may feel alone as if no one understands, but this is not so. There's a reason there are *numerous* support groups. There are groups for alcoholics, battered persons, rape victims, overeaters, and just plain ole groups galore. If you find yourself not fitting into one group, chances are, you'll fit into another. Don't view needing a support group as a sign of weakness or something to be ashamed of, rather, view it as an opportunity to awaken your senses. During their time in a support group, many have found out interesting things about their nature and way of being. Many have experienced a jolting of their senses. It's pretty inevitable.

It's my sincerest hope and prayer you'll use this book in more ways than one. Let all the words contained within, serve as a reminder, an eye-opener, a comic relief, and a "back-to-earth" guide. Too often, we allow ourselves to wallow for quite some time in self-pity. Let this not be so! Life tossing us like a rag doll is not GOD's intentions. Sure, have your pity party, but remember, all parties come to an end. Know when to send your guests home!

Our triumph over the enemy, a healthy mind, and a thriving environment, are all a part of GOD's ultimate plan. Therefore, grabbing the bull by its' horns is just the first of many steps, but it's not enough to suffice! We *must* employ what we've learned. We must be courageous! Sooner than later we must tackle those very issues utilizing our strengths as leverage to conquer our weaknesses. Inadvertently, in so doing, we build upon our strengths.

As you read each epistle, I pray you will realize there *are* real devastations afflicting so many. It's my prayer that after you read each epistle, you'll realize there are others who are, who have or who will soon face some of the most horrific battles one could encounter. I pray that, upon completion of this book, such devastations will no longer be foreign to you. I pray when you're at your lowest point, your mind will rehash memories of *these* epistles to help abate feelings of hopelessness and destitution. I pray each epistle will help you put things into proper perspective.

Some conversations (prayers) are jovial and lighthearted while others are intense and at times demonstrate a lack of total reverence to Abba, the Most-High Almighty GOD. You'll find some words to be nonexistent and may come across as plain ole babblings! Those babblings were intentionally included to suit the situation of the individual praying. It's important to note that none of the prayers are meant to be offensive. These prayers simply display the countless ways in which one may pray to/petition, the Father.

Hopefully while reading each epistle, you will become engulfed in every word and you will view life through the eyes of your brethren –black or white, short or tall, male or female, rich or poor. As you read, I pray you will be able to empathize with the pain, experience the humor, appreciate the innocence, but most of all, relate to the humaneness and vulnerability of each prayer. Allow yourself the freedom to experience various emotions. Take full advantage of the purpose of each petition because each one *is* meant to move you. Some may humor you, others scorch you, but overall, I believe each prayer *will* provoke the stirring of emotions in you. These are deep-seated thoughts from the minds and hearts of real people. These are their cries and unspoken words behind each teardrop.

There is *no* special way to communicate with GOD. Therefore, each prayer presents in various ways. Some prayers may seem offensive to some readers. Beloved, please know it is *not* my intention to offend or belittle anyone of you. It is my mission to provide words that will cause all readers of this book to experience a sense of relief.

Epistles to Abba: Letters from the Heart will aid in strengthening a new Christian's walk with the Lord, provide support for the seasoned Christian, and pique the interest of the non-believer. It is my earnest prayer this book will be received by each reader according to their needs. Beloved, Abba GOD *is* real. He sits on His throne watching, waiting, listening for, and to, and addressing our prayers. For we *are* His beloved children. We are made from dust crafted by the only Alpha and Omega – GOD Almighty, Abba Himself. <u>Ecclesiastes 3:20</u> [20]*"All go unto one place; all are of the dust, and all turn to dust again."* <u>Psalm 103:13-14</u> ~ [13]*"Like as a father pitieth his children, so the Lord pitieth them that fear him. [14]For he knoweth our frame; he remembereth that we are dust."*

Finally, now that we've discussed the essence of prayer and praying, let's talk structure. The book's epistles are structured in the manner in which a letter may be written to a friend. Each Epistle (letter) is numbered as such: **Epistle No.** followed by the respective numbered epistle/letter/prayer. Example: the 5th Epistle epistle/letter/prayer in the book is denoted as, **Epistle No. 5**. This is followed by the salutation **Dear GOD**, which is the opening address in each prayer to the Father a.k.a. Abba. Next is the body of the epistle, this is the actual prayer, followed by the valediction and signature of the person praying. For example, if the person is a smoker wanting to stop smoking and prays to ask GOD to help him/her quit smoking, the prayer would end with the person's signature as **Smoker**. Finally, after the signature of the prayer, you'll find GOD's active role or nature while listening to the prayer. For example, if the person has recently lost a loved one, is depressed and crying, the name used to represent one of the Father's attributes/characteristics might be, **GOD the Healer**. This would indicate GOD as actively listening and actively healing the individual as they pray.

Disclaimer: I am in no way saying GOD only begins working on behalf of an individual once they start praying. ABSOLUTELY NOT! I cannot stress this enough. It is most imperative you understand that GOD works in mysterious ways and He works according to how *He* sees fit. His ways are higher than our ways and His thoughts are higher than our thoughts. GOD is always aware of everything at every time. Remember, GOD knows our thoughts even before we have them! GOD knew everything about us before we even knew ourselves!

Amen!   Psalm 139:1- 4 ~ *[1] "O lord, thou hast searched me, and known me. [2] "Thou knowest my downsitting and mine uprising, thou understandest my thought afar off. [3]Thou compassest my path and my lying down, and art acquainted with all my ways. [4]For there is not a word in my tongue, but, lo, O Lord, thou knowest it altogether."*

The most salient point here is, prayer is simply communication with GOD.

Prayers are said in various ways, presents in varied styles, and offered in numerous languages. No matter what, incessantly practice these 3 points:

1. Never lie during prayer! Be sincere. GOD already knows *all* your thoughts.
   ~ John 4:24 *[24] "God is a Spirit: and they that worship him must worship him in spirit and in truth."*

2. Never pray to be seen. GOD does not honor that!
   ~ Matthew 6:5 reads, *[5] "And when thou prayest, thou shalt not be as the hypocrites are: for they love to pray standing in the synagogues and in the corners of the streets, that they may be seen of men. Verily I say unto you, They have their reward."*

And most importantly,

3. Never stop praying! You'll stop communicating with GOD. In the book of 1 Thessalonians 5:16-18 we read, [16] *"Rejoice evermore.* [17] *Pray without ceasing.* [18] *In every thing give thanks: for this is the will of God in Christ Jesus concerning you."* Psalm 102:17 states,[17] *"He will regard the prayer of the destitute, and not despise their prayer."* Philippians 4:6 says,[6] *"Be careful for nothing; but in every thing by prayer and supplication with thanksgiving let your requests be made known unto God."*

Now, as you experience some of life's most profound realities, sit back, laugh heartily, have a good cry, or do both while embracing the stirring inside you!

May GOD be your guide and His angels walk by your side. Blessings and love.

Sophia Mattis,

GOD the Holy Trinity

"And seeing the multitudes, he went up into a mountain: and when he was set, his disciples came unto him: [2] *And he opened his mouth, and taught them, saying,* [3] *Blessed are the poor in spirit: for theirs is the kingdom of heaven.* [4] *Blessed are they that mourn: for they shall be comforted.* [5] *"Blessed are the meek: for they shall inherit the earth.* [6] *Blessed are they which do hunger and*

thirst after righteousness: for they shall be filled. [7] Blessed are the merciful: for they shall obtain mercy. [8] Blessed are the pure in heart: for they shall see God. [9] Blessed are the peacemakers: for they shall be called the children of God. [10] Blessed are they which are persecuted for righteousness' sake: for theirs is the kingdom of heaven. [11] Blessed are ye, when men shall revile you, and persecute you, and shall say all manner of evil against you falsely, for my sake. [12] Rejoice, and be exceeding glad: for great is your reward in heaven: for so persecuted they the prophets which were before you. [13] Ye are the salt of the earth: but if the salt have lost his savour, wherewith shall it be salted? it is thenceforth good for nothing, but to be cast out, and to be trodden under foot of men." ~ Matthew 5:1-13

The Epistles

"After this manner therefore pray ye:

Our Father which art in heaven, Hallowed be thy name. Thy kingdom come, Thy will be done in earth, as it is in heaven. Give us this day our daily bread. And forgive us our debts, as we forgive our debtors. And lead us not into temptation, but deliver us from evil: For thine is the kingdom, and the power, and the glory, forever. Amen."

~ Matthew 6-9-13 ~

Epistle No. 1

Dear GOD,

Good morning.

Tired

GOD the Giver of Life
Life

> [24] *"This is the day which the LORD hath made; we will rejoice and be glad in it."* ~ Psalm 118:24

Epistle No. 2

Dear GOD,

Why'd I stay in a relationship for eleven years only to end up being by myself?! Yeah, I know I was the one who called it off, but I only did that because it wasn't a healthy relationship. I mean, he wasn't a bad guy or anything, but he just never put into the relationship as much as I thought he should've.

"I kept you from being afflicted by a disease, taught you the power of commitment, and allowed your mind to be settled so you could focus on school and those are the minor things." ~ GOD

Why am I always struggling with my weight? If I would have never taken that stupid birth control method, my metabolism wouldn't be all screwy. I would be ok today, but no, I just had to take that stupid method! I read all the side effects and I even asked the doctor his opinion. Everything said green light. Well, there went that!

"For starters, I caused you to become an avid exerciser, which kept the stress off you and your health in check. I caused you to have time for meditation on the pier so you would hear My voice." ~ GOD

Why did I get put on the waiting list for a top-ranking school, but I chose not to go?
They told me they wouldn't be able to accept me until the following year. I wasn't going to wait for them; I decided to go to that other school. Yeah, I knew I'd be very far from my family, but I figured I'd get over it since I only had a few months to do.

"I allowed you to build a stronger relationship with Me, to grow, to travel the world, to experience various cultures, to enjoy excellent weather year-round; to be free. That was just the beginning." ~ GOD

Why am I not married and why don't I have children yet? I've been faithful and have been trying to be obedient, I'm even celibate! Lord, don't you think it's time? I love children and family, they're important to me, but still, I'm single. Yes, I know it's by choice, but that's only because I haven't come across that man who I think is equally yoked with me.

"I gave you time to write this book, enjoy the single life, live pretty much obligation free, learn from other people's marital and familial mistakes, remove the rose-colored glasses, and become fixed in your mind as to what things truly matter in life. And I'm merely skimming the surface. ~ GOD"

Why am I broke? I mean cut me some slack here Lord. I don't even have a penny! Ok, so that's a lie. Yeah, I know I have some loose change floating around, but that's not real money. I can't travel or go to those eateries I used to enjoy. You know I'm a big movie buff, and movies haven't been an option. Oh yeah, that's right, You did get me a pass for free movies every Tuesday. Well, I haven't been able to help my loved ones or better yet Lord, forget all of that; I can't even get the basics – ice cream! Yeah, I know that's not essential, but I love it, and as You can see, it loves me too. It makes my heart go pitter-patter. Don't You like it when my heart goes pitter-patter?

"I caused you to truly realize the value of money, appreciate the smaller things in life, experience what the less fortunate endure, develop a determination to practice excellence with money management, and most of all I was, doing a great work in and through you!
This work will cause ALL the glory, the honor, and the praise to be given unto Me – Your GOD! And that's just to list a few things." ~ GOD

Ungrateful Sophie

GOD the Sad

[13] "For it is God which worketh in you both to will and to do of his good pleasure. [14] Do all things without murmurings and disputings: [15] That ye may be blameless and harmless, the sons of God, without rebuke, in the midst of a crooked and perverse nation, among whom ye shine as lights in the world; [16] Holding forth the word of life; that I may rejoice in the day of Christ, that I have not run in vain, neither laboured in vain." ~ Philippiaans 2:13-15

Epistle No. 3

Dear GOD,

Listen, I kind of feel awkward having to say this, but I guess I better spit it out before You hear it from someone else. I've been invited to a party and the host told me I can bring anyone except You. Ok, ok, she didn't say except You. Come to think of it, she didn't say I couldn't bring anyone. She said I have an open invitation to invite whoever I want.

Well, buddy, here's the thing, You know you're my best bud. Normally I invite You to everything and I lean on You for everything, but just this one time, I think I have to do this alone. Here's the thing, this party is a hip party. The best of the best will be there. You know, the who's who of who. The crème de la crème! This party is for all the heavyweights, no lightweights allowed. What's that… yeah, I know, You won the *Most Influential Person of All Time* award. Of course, I know! I was there! I was the one who reminded You when You were boo – whooing, remember. I felt like I was at the Oscars. Anyhow, listen, don't get all sentimental on me. All I'm saying is I can't bring You along. Don't make this harder than it has to be. It's just a stupid party that's gonna be filled with a whole bunch of stuffy people. It ain't gonna be no real shin ding. Picture a group of penguins sliding around on the ice. What? Why'd I use penguins? Well because they're dressed in black and white, the same colors the men will be dressed in. As for the women, it's pretty much the same since it's a black and white affair. They'll greet each other just as the French do, with kisses. Oh no, that's forbidden. That's not posh. They won't hug because that seems too, uh, let's just say, hugs don't display proper etiquette. Then they'll all be gliding across the dance floor, all stuffy, too afraid to make one misstep. They must be perfectly choreographed for every song that plays. They'll chuckle at the most hilarious jokes instead of being in stitches, and they'll eat finger food just to wet their palates. They'll guzzle down gallons of alcohol within reach to ease the hunger pangs and then begin making rude remarks to anyone in sight. Well, no, of course, I'm not saying every *single* one of them will behave this way, but I promise, it'll be the majority. The atmosphere is gonna be so cold, You'll think You're in Antarctica!

GOD, trust me, this is *not* a party You want to attend. You just wouldn't fit in. You're just too…well, You know, too religious. You walk around with that holier than thou kind of attitude and I just don't know if they'll be able to stomach that. Heck, I mean, half the times, I can't even stomach it, but what are friends for.

Oh, come on, don't go getting all bent out of shape about this. It's just a silly little party. Why do You care so much about going anyway? I mean, why do You have to be a part of everything I do? Frankly, it's a bit annoying to have You wanting to tag along everywhere I go. You want to be in everything I do, say, and think. That can be such a burden at times. The last time I checked, I was born alone. We're not conjoined twins! Guess what, we're not twins at all! Why do You always have to make things so hard? You *always* make things seem more drastic than it is. You're so melodramatic. I mean goodness, You make everything seem like it's life or death! You see, this is exactly why I don't want to take You. Better yet, this is exactly why I'm *not* taking You! Everything with You is set in stone! You never think for one moment, just *one* moment, that things can change, and that they may just change?

Listen, I don't wanna fight. I've had enough of this. Stop trying to make me feel bad. For heaven's sake, stop with the guilt trip! Enough already I don't wanna be in a tug of war with You. Can't we just all get along? You know you're my oldest and dearest friend. I trust You with my life, but there are just times when I have to step out on my own. By the way, will You make sure I get there safe?

User

GOD the Provider

⁷ "Be not deceived; God is not mocked: for whatsoever a man soweth, that shall he also reap." ~ Galatians 6:7

Epistle No. 4

Dear GOD,

Can you believe they think I don't have a mind of my own!? Yeah, yeah, yeah, I know, that's the word on the street. They think I listen to everything You say and that I'm Your puppet. They think I allow You to pull all my strings. They even said I'm like an elevator because I allow You to push my buttons and I just go along with whatever You tell me. The nerve of those phony, pathetic, spineless, poor excuse for a human being! They didn't even have the nerve to say it to my face. They huddle together like a pack of wolves just waiting to see who they can devour! How dare they! I mean, this is absolutely preposterous! Well, I'm not gonna sit back and take this kind of abuse! All these accusations, they're just not accurate. Quite frankly, they're the furthest thing from the truth. What do they know? They don't know me! They haven't walked a mile in my shoes. They haven't gone through *my* trials, and *my* tribulations. I repeat, *my* trials and tribulations! I know, they're all just jealous! They sit around watching me, waiting for the perfect opportunity to criticize me. I mean, what is it about me? Why are they so curious about what I do? Why do they just lie and wait to devour me? This is a true example of character assassination! What did I ever do to them, I just tried to love them? What? Yeah, I know, I said, they don't even know me and I don't know them. Some of the folks who gathered around used to come around to hang out with me when I was flying high, and life was good. Since I lost all, I had, now they're acting like they never knew me.

Ok, it's one thing when people I don't know talk about me, but quite another when people I know talk mess about me! They're the ones I would expect to stand up for me. I mean, you should see them. They gather around laughing and talking, eating and drinking, dancing, and doing all those worldly things until they see me coming. Then they simmer down and begin whispering amongst themselves. They act as if like the very sight of me is repulsive! The audacity! *I* was the one who loaned them money to pay for their kids to go to private school. *I* was the one who bought them the fancy car You see them driving all over town. *I* was the one who was there waiting in the hospital all night. *I* had to use my pull to assure they got the best of the best to perform surgery. *I* was even the one who paid their mortgage for umm, let's see, umpteen years so they would have a place to rest! *I* was the one who gave them all those gift cards to the Supermart so they could buy food *and* their necessities. *I* was the one who put in the good word, so they got that management position at that fortune 500 company. *I* was the one who saw to it their names were cleared when folks tried scandalizing them. *I* was the one who cooked every day when I got home from work *completely* exhausted. *I* was the one who kept that secret. *I* was the one who didn't turn them in when they robbed that house! Whoops, I guess that's no longer a secret huh. Oh well, I did my best, I kept it a secret for the past 12 years. I mean how much more can one ask. Gosh, I feel kind of bad about that. Now everyone's gonna know what they did. Oh well, the same way they turned their backs on me and showed no sort of loyalty, that's just payback. Now they see what disloyalty feels like. Huh, please, I don't care, I'm human like them. Oh well, time to move on.

Used

GOD the Faithful

[9] *"And let us not be weary in well doing: for in due season we shall reap, if we faint not. [10] As we have therefore opportunity, let us do good unto all men, especially unto them who are of the household of faith." ~ Galatians 6-9-10*

Epistle No. 5

Dear GOD,

What have I done? I didn't mean to do it. I really didn't. If only he would've stopped while he was ahead, all of this wouldn't have spun out of control. GOD, my heart's racing. What am I supposed to do now? I've seriously made a mess of things. Mom always told me to watch my temper. She warned me *all* the time. I thought I had gotten my temper under control. For sure I did. I never realized I still had it in me. I never thought it would ever get the best of me.

Ok, why are You interrupting me? I'm trying to tell You how I made a major booboo and how I'm in a major crisis and You're cutting me off. CUT ME SOME SLACK HERE! I'm trying to get to the point! I'm getting there! You talk about me not having patience, what's the deal with You?! Alright, You know what, I better just tell You now so You can get off my back once and for all!

I beat a guy so bad, he had to be rushed to the hospital and worst yet, the word is he might not make it. He's in critical condition. Oh my goodness!!!!! How am I supposed to tell You the whole story if You keep cutting me off! I'm trying to calm down, but You're just adding fuel to the fire every time You tell me to relax. How am I supposed to relax when I know this guy might die and it's all because of me?! I'm here tossing and turning because of my stupid temper. My childish behavior got me in this mess. I'm thinking of how You always tell me it's ok to get angry but be careful not to sin. I know, I know, I know. Oh my goodness gracious do I know! How can I not know? You are a constant reminder of how imperfect I am. Yeah, yeah, yeah, I know You're not here to badger me or to make me feel bad. I know You're only telling me the truth. Sometimes the truth is an offense. The truth hurts sometimes, You know.

GOD, what am I supposed to do now? I'm in a whole heap of mess. Here's the thing, no one knows I was the assailant. They're out there looking for the offender. I ran after everything happened. It was dark and we were in a desolate place. We were getting on good, walking back to our cars when all of a sudden, this dude decides to paint me as a hothead. It all started when I stepped into a hole, twisted my ankle and I collapsed into a puddle of sewage water. I ruined my plush new suit! My ankle was throbbing, and on the embarrassment scale of 1-10, I brought in a whopping 20!! The group walking ahead of us heard the noise, turned around, and saw me collapsing to the ground! They belted out the loudest laugh I've ever heard! I was furious! I got up, with no help from my loser friend, and began to hop towards the car. Oh yeah, did I forget to mention I was swearing up, down, and all around?! I was a little intoxicated and I think that's what caused the loud vulgarities coming out my mouth. My so-called friend kept telling me to calm down. He felt I was out of control. He said I was blowing things out of proportion. Why'd he feel the need to become my pacifier? That just triggered a more deadly fire since I was in so much pain and embarrassed. I was a mess! And I mean that, literally and figuratively. So, of course, I started yelling at him! I'll admit, I said some pretty harsh things that weren't called for, and naturally, he retaliated. After all, I was the one who had the right to be angry, not him. I was the one who just experienced a horrific ordeal, not to mention the tremendous amount of pain in my ankle. I told him to forget about it and he wouldn't, so I just kept on going. Then he said the unthinkable. I won't dare repeat what he said, but that's when I swung at him! It's not like I'm stronger than him or anything, but it was just my bad misfortune, as I was swinging, I stumbled, socked him good and he lost his balance. As he fell, I fell on top of him and started to pound on him. I only did that because he started to swing back. Why didn't he just restrain me? Had he done that, none of this would have happened. I would have stopped whilst I was ahead. So, there we were, swinging like wild beasts, and at one point, I grabbed his head and bashed it into the cement. I only did it once, but I guess one time was enough. He stopped swinging and just laid there still. At one point, I thought he was dead. If it weren't for the fact, he was still breathing, I would have sworn I killed him.

Oh GOD, what am I supposed to do now, I got up and ran like a coward! I called the police from the payphone and then hopped in my car and sped off! It's only a miracle I didn't kill myself trying to get home. I was frantic! I was intoxicated and speeding. I'm surprised no cops pulled me over. I prayed and prayed *all* the way home. When I finally made it through the front door, I was such a nervous wreck, I forgot to turn the alarm off. Next thing I know, the cops were at the front door asking me if everything is ok. It's not like I live in one of those neighborhoods where the security company calls you to check if all is well. I live in Prestige Pines where the cops are at your door within seconds! Nevertheless, I told the officers everything's ok and I was just rushing to the restroom. One of them looked at me, took a deep breath, and said, "Are you sure you're ok? It seems as if you've had a bit much to drink." There I was, slurring my speech. I was pretty much stammering, wobbling with bloodshot eyes, torn, soaking wet clothes, matted bloody hair, and breath strong enough to make anyone tipsy! What was I supposed to say? It's a good thing in my neighborhood, the cops don't push too hard, which was a good thing for me. If they do, they know their butts will be out of a job! So based on that, all I had to say was, "I said I'm fine and I was rushing to the restroom," and off they went. What a relief! Hey, are you listening? You haven't said a word the whole time.

Fearful Venter

GOD the Listener

> [10] *"Fear thou not; for I am with thee: be not dismayed; for I am thy God: I will strengthen thee; yea, I will help thee; yea, I will uphold thee with the right hand of my righteousness." ~ Isaiah 41:10*

> [6] *"Be careful for nothing; but in every thing by prayer and supplication with thanksgiving let your requests be made known unto God. [7] And the peace of God, which passeth all understanding, shall keep your hearts and minds through Christ Jesus." ~ Philippians 4:6*

Epistle No. 6

Dear GOD,

Urgh! Why does this stupid phone keep ringing? It's been ringing off the hook all day. I'm trying to focus here! I mean, for Pete's sake, the phone's been ringing off the hook! It's those bill collectors again. They're the only ones that call all day, every day. I mean, they even call on Sundays. I know, I know, if I were in the church, it wouldn't bother me as much because I wouldn't be home half the day to hear the phone continuously ringing. I know it's those bill collectors because everyone else calls me after 9 pm when they know I'm settled in. I mean anyone can call now because I'm permanently settled in, I have no job! Yeah, thanks GOD for Your condolences. I appreciate that, but unfortunately, that ain't gonna pay the bills. My company looked as if they were making a turn for the better, but instead, they took a turn for the worst. It's a great company, and the people there are an awesome bunch. I wouldn't dare say a bad word against anyone of them. They've been nothing but good to me.

What's that? Oh yeah, I remember her. She's the gal who complained *all* the time. She drove *everyone* at work absolutely bonkers, but even she was alright. She was a bit quirky, neurotic, eclectic, and a little bizarre, to say the least, but all and all she meant no harm. As long as everything around her was organic, animal cruelty-free, smoke-free, germ-free, fat-free, and just plain ole' *free*, then she was cool. It only took me a month to figure out her pet peeves, and then I was in the clear. After that, she never swung on my nerves again. You know GOD, I think if more people took time to understand her and just let her be, they too wouldn't have been troubled.

Although we're in the same predicament, I feel she has it worse. Oh yes, they laid her off too. Yes indeedie, they sure did. I know, she must be ripping her hair out. With 5 kids, a mortgage, a disabled husband, elderly parents, and her struggle with Lupus, she probably feels like all is lost. Her meds alone cost an arm and a leg and let's not even talk about home care for her parents. That's a doozie for yah! Let's not forget the 5 mouths she has to feed. All of them are mere tots. They can't go out and fend for themselves. Her plate is full.

Well, what do you think? Should I bring a couple of bags of food to her tomorrow? I don't have much here, but I think I can spare a few canned goods. I even had some extra meat I bought to the potluck, which, by the way, never happened. Yeah, that's what I'll do. First thing tomorrow, I'll rummage through the pantry and the fridge to see what I can spare. I know I don't have a lot, and without a job, I definitely have to ration things out, but I mean what am I supposed to do. I can't just sit here knowing she has all those mouths to feed. What kind of person wouldn't help? What kind of a person would I be if *I* didn't help?

Ring . . .ring . . . ring . . . ring. Hello, you've reached me, but unfortunately, I'm not available to answer the phone. Please leave a message after the beep and I'll be sure to get back to you. Bye for now and have a blessed day. Beep. "Hello, this is Ace Govella, of Govella, Klien, and Hetching. I am the attorney handling the Smithburg estates that belonged to your great uncle. I've been trying to reach you and it seems I keep missing you. I'm calling on behalf of Mr. Smithburg to inform you that he has passed away. He's named you in his will. Please give me a call at 555-555-5555 at your earliest convenience so we may further discuss this matter, it would be greatly appreciated. Thank you." Click.

Proper Perspective

GOD the Architect

[10] *"But the God of all grace, who hath called us unto his eternal glory by Christ Jesus, after that ye have suffered a while, make you perfect, stablish, strengthen, settle you.* [11] *To him be glory and dominion for ever and ever. Amen." ~ 1 Peter 5:10-11*

Epistle No. 7

Dear GOD,

All I remember is this: Our Father, who stood by the seashore. No, no, no, that's not right. I know mother used to tell me to say these prayers when I was young, but I can't seem to remember them. If only I could remember at least one of them. Ok, I'll give it another shot. The Lord is my Shepherd I shall be obedient. No, that's not it either. Wait a minute. Oh goodness – get away from me! Father, bless me for I have sinned. Hail Mary, Ms. Mary Mack, Mack, Mack all dressed in black. Wait, that's definitely not right either!!!!! Oh GOD. Oh dear GOD. Oh GOD. Please have mercy on me. I need Your help. Oh GOD, please help me. Get them away from me. They're tormenting me. They torment me night and day. I can't eat, I can't sleep, I can't do anything without them terrifying me! Oh GOD, there they go again. Please save me. My mother warned me of these demons. Why didn't I believe her? Jesus, please, help me. Get away from me! Leave me alone! What do you want with me?! That hurts. You're hurting me. Oh GOD no . . . don't do that! Stop doing that to me. Oh GOD! Oh my GOD. Oh heaven. Someone, help me! Someone, please help me. Father, Father! Lord. Jesus, have mercy on me. Please forgive me. I'm sorry. Please don't leave me here. JESUS! If You get me out of here, I promise I'll listen to You from now on. I'll never forsake You. Please, JESUS, get me out of here! Jesus. Jesus. Jesus.

Then suddenly, a bright light appeared, and I saw Your hand Jesus. Oh Jesus, You came to save me. Please get me out of here! Please don't leave me. Don't leave me Jesus. Don't ever leave me. I'm so sorry.

Atheist

GOD the Merciful

> [19] *"Thou believest that there is one God; thou doest well: the devils also believe, and tremble." ~ James 2:19*

Epistle No. 8

"Dear GOD," John managed to get out before Lucas interrupted him. "Huh, oh please, who calls on *a* GOD," Lucas said sarcastically. I'm not calling on no GOD! Better you than me cause you know I'm not calling on no GOD. Why would I call on *something* or *someone* I'm not sure is…? Well, you know what I mean. What am I saying? Obviously, that's just sheer stupidity. Don't be offended. We're adults, so let's analyze this like two levelheaded adults. Let's look at this with a rational mind. Have you ever seen this "GOD" you talk about? That's what I thought. How could you be all fanatical about something you haven't seen? You're not even sure if this GOD you talk about exist. Clearly, I'm the sane one here. Insanity plagues so many people, including my friend. I must say, I'm a bit worried about you John. I've never heard you talk like that. I mean, you were always the most brilliant student in *all* our classes. Our studies came so easy to you. I had to work pretty gosh darn hard just to pass. I guess all that studying has gone to your head. It's made you a bit cuckoo. I'm not trying to be disrespectful here, but dude all I have to say is, "One who flew over the cuckoo's nest."

"Dear GOD," again, John attempted to pray.

"Would You stop, Lucas spewed." Just stop it! You sound silly. Unless you're calling this GOD down to earth so I can see Him, then this is *all* a bunch of crap! I can tell you this, if your GOD appears and I see this GOD of yours, then I'll *know* for sure that a GOD exists. I mean, who or what are you calling on? Listen, here's the deal, here's a proposition for you. If you can show me *your* so-called GOD right now, I'll become a Christian. I will know for sure there *is* a 'GOD'. Hey man, I'm not totally against this belief you have, but I only deal with facts. Unless you show me proof, I'm not going to believe *a GOD* exists." I'm just not sure if there is a GOD. There may or may not be a GOD. I need some form of tangible evidence. Show me the proof and we'll take it from there. Science can't prove existence and religion can't provide any evidence. There's no way to know the truth until you die! Wouldn't you agree? I mean, I just don't know if GOD exists. I'm not gonna say: if I can't see it, feel it, touch it, smell it, or experience it, I'm not game. I just don't know. Maybe you can prove it to me another way.

Man listen, John, you know me, I'm a cool cat. I'm a laid-back dude. I'm just on that pendulum and I'm not trying to frazzle *anyone's* nerves. Hey! Hey! John, slow down! Hold your horses. I'm the neutral guy, *remember*. So don't go beatin' me up. I just figured

I'd remind you of that before I end up unconscious. I'm a lover, not a fighter. I just think all of this is pointless. I mean if you can't prove it and if you can't deny it, then what's the point? What's the big deal? It's not like I claim to be an atheist or anything. Give me some credit here. At least I'm not blatantly denying the existence of *a* GOD! You know I have a problem with commitment. I don't see anything wrong with having a noncommittal kind of attitude. I can't know for *sure* if *a* GOD exists or not and neither can you. Face the facts, you can only experience things in *this* tangible world. You can't experience anything outside of it. John, where's your brain?! It seems like you've lost it! I don't know about you man; I'm starting to wonder about you.

You see what I'm talking about? Here's a perfect example. If there *is* a GOD, why are we still walking in the rain and no one's stopped to offer us a ride? It's raining cats and dogs and people are just zooming by. They don't even care to help us. Wouldn't this GOD of yours make *someone* stop to give us a ride or something?

John began praying, "Dear GOD, please stop the rain. Make it hold up until we get to shelter. And Lord, even if You choose not to stop the rain, do me a favor and at least stop my skeptical friend from yapping. The yapping – awe the yapping Lord. I can only stomach but so much of it, including his disbelief. Oh, wait a minute, correction, I got that wrong, it's his lack of knowledge that's keeping him in a fog, not his disbelief. I know Lord, sarcasm, it's not becoming. I don't mean to be hypocritical, but Father, will You please make the sun come out. Let the sunshine so bright no one would have ever thought it rained. GOD, please stop this rain, I'm freezing. And GOD, please stop this rain so Lucas will start believing in You. In Jesus' name, I pray. Amen."

"Woah John, check it out," Lucas said. Look, a few feet ahead of us. Over there in the valley. Dude, that's a humungous rainbow! As a matter of fact, what happened to the rain?"

"Thank You Father," John humbly whispered with cherry-colored cheeks.

Agnostic

GOD Who Answers Prayers

[10] *"Be still, and know that I am God: I will be exalted among the heathen, I will be exalted in the earth. [11] The LORD of hosts is with us; the God of Jacob is our refuge. Selah." ~ Psalm 46:10-11*

Epistle No. 9

Dear GOD,

I love You; I thank You; I need You. In Jesus' name, I pray. Amen.

Sorry Lord . . . I'm late, but I just wanted to say, I love You. Gotta go.

Late

GOD of Understanding

[37] *"Jesus said unto him, Thou shalt love the Lord thy God with all thy heart, and with all thy soul, and with all thy mind." ~ Matthew 22:37*

Epistle No. 10

Dear GOD,

What am I, chopped liver? I've been praying and praying and praying forever now. Lord, I've been asking You to send the right person into my life, but still nothing. I mean Lord, what am I doing wrong? I've prayed and prayed and prayed and still, nothing! You said we're supposed to ask and so we shall receive. You said we're supposed to seek and so we shall find. You said, knock and it will be opened up unto to us. You said we're supposed to have faith and that faith without works, is dead. You say that patience is a virtue. Oh, wait a minute, that patience thing, scratch that. That one was from someone else. Well, I know for sure, You said, we're supposed to put our trust in You for You will never forsake us nor leave us, but still. . . nada. Oh yes, I remember, You said, You are good unto them that wait for You, to the soul that seeketh You. Yup, I remember that scripture, it's in Lamentations 3:25. Grandma use to say this to us *all* the time. Let me see, bear with me as I review my checklist. I've prayed and nothing. I've asked – um excuse me – that would be prayer, and still nothing. I've sought out people and bingo You got it, nothing. I've knocked until I couldn't knock anymore. Oh Lord, hold on, I have a quick question, this one threw me through a loop. For clarification purposes, was I supposed to knock at Your door, my prospective mate's door, the car door . . . um, exactly which door was I supposed to knock on? Ok, I'll give You that one. Hehe.

I thought I had the faith thing locked down. I mean, I've been praying for years, and I've gone out making myself available just in case person right shows up but guess again. You got it, nothing! Oh, and Lord, I can't quite recall Your words of wisdom when it comes to patience, but Lord, wouldn't You say I've been very patient? I mean, cut me some slack here! I think we can both agree, I've waited long enough. So here goes Lord, I'm gonna try this faith thing *one* more time and Lord if You don't come through then, I'm just gonna die! You know what, I'm gonna try the whole praying, asking, knocking, and seeking thingy all over again and this time, I'm expecting answers. Hey Mr., isn't it in Genesis where You said, "It's not good that man should be alone?" Yup, You sure did?

I know I'm in school double full-time, plus I'm holding down a "so-called job," wait does double full-time even make any sense? Oh well, whatever! I mean, what does that have to do with anything? A relationship won't derail me. Who, Toni? What about Toni? I *know* she dropped out of school. I don't know what went wrong with her relationship. All I know is, one day there was joy, the next day sorrow, then stress, disappointment, resentment, fury, and guilt. Oh my goodness, it went on and on. I'm tired even talking about it! I know she was depressed, and then the last thing I heard was she dropped out of school. All that time, money, hard work and not to mention, a childhood dream, all down the drain. That's unfortunate. I feel so bad every time I think of her story. Toni was such a good kind-hearted person. You don't find many people like that anymore. Well, what can I say? Her relationship was a rollercoaster ride. Can we just *say* that doomsday doesn't come close to doing justice to her dysfunctional hook-up? If that's what they call a relationship, I'll pass. I tell You Lord, if that were me, I don't know what I would've done. Thank goodness I'm not in Toni's shoes.

Alright now GOD, don't go getting me off track. Let's get back to business. What about that hand-picked mate you promised me?

Clueless

GOD the Omniscient

[5] "Trust in the LORD with all thine heart; and lean not unto thine own understanding." ~ Proverbs 3:5

Epistle No. 11

Dear GOD,

It's an honor and a privilege to serve You. You are the most upstanding and upright person I have ever known! Sometimes I forget to tell You how fantastic You are and how much Your friendship means to me. I know it's hard to say how I feel all the *time* because I have done *so* many things to offend You, that sorry is no longer enough. I don't deserve a friend like You, but no matter what LORD, You always stick by me. I curse, I swear, I say things I don't mean out of anger towards You, nevertheless, You are always there for me.

I think it's important for people to tell each other how much they appreciate one another. Although this has been said by countless authors, mothers, fathers, and people of all sorts, I feel the need to say it again. No Sir, I'm not trying to reinvent the wheel. Obviously, I'm no Thomas Edison. I'm just trying to add another spoke to its frame.

I don't want this to come across all mushy or like I'm begging to be Your friend. I just want You to know how greatly I appreciate You. Please don't turn Your back on me. Please don't leave me. Please don't stop talking to me. You know You're the only one who can tolerate my insanity, my insensitivity, my narcissism, my "It's all about me" attitude without batting an eye. Please never stop feeding my egotistical attitude by telling me how much You love me even when I am being … well you know, let's just say, not so nice. I mean come on, let's be real here, who else could and would put up with my attitude? I can't even stand my attitude! When I act hostile, sometimes I just say, "What the heck is that all about?" It's pretty freaky if I must say so myself.

Ok, ok, I know, I always make things about me. It's not all about me. I'm saying this to You so by right it should be all about You and Your greatness. No, but seriously, on a serious note, what in the world would I do without You?! Hum, let's see? Well, of course, I would go on living a boring lonely, defeated life. I would wake up in the mornings and still have to face another day afraid and defenseless. I would probably still be eager to find a mate and get married. What an empty marriage that would be. Well, surely family would be the answer – a loveless family that is. I would still have an amazing career. Yeah, a career that lacks growth and satisfaction. Well, I would still be promised death, that's one thing I know for sure, an eternity of separation from You. MY GOD!!!!! What would I do without You?!

Grateful

GOD the Savior

"Make a joyful noise unto the LORD, all ye lands. ² Serve the LORD with gladness: come before his presence with singing. ³ Know ye that the LORD he is God: it is he that hath made us, and not we ourselves; we are his people, and the sheep of his pasture. ⁴ Enter into his gates with thanksgiving, and into his courts with praise: be thankful unto him, and bless his name. ⁵ For the LORD is good; his mercy is everlasting; and his truth endureth to all generations." ~ Psalm 100

Epistle No. 12

Dear GOD,

Hi. I love You.

Remembrance

GOD the Delighted

[27] *"And he answering said, Thou shalt love the Lord thy God with all thy heart, and with all thy soul, and with all thy strength, and with all thy mind; and thy neighbour as thyself." ~ Luke 100:27*

Epistle No. 13

Dear GOD,

GOD, are You crying? A little birdie told me You may be wallowing in a pool of tears. You know I hate seeing You cry. It makes my heart weak. It's bad enough my heart is only but so strong. I mean, what are You trying to do to me here? If I didn't know better, I would think You're trying to kill me! I would think You are trying to give me a heart attack. NO! CPR won't work for me; I don't want anyone putting their lips on me and heaven knows I sure don't need a novice crushing my ribs! All those inexperienced folks out there who call their selves doctors, nurses, paramedics, or whatever fancy pants name they decide to slap on what they do are so incompetent. You know as well as I do, that half of them are drunkards, while the others need medication for their "GOD complex." Whoops, there I go again, off on a tangent, just blabbing about whatever I feel is riding my nerves.

I'm the best person to talk to for consolation. I do a pretty awful job at consoling myself much less consoling someone else. I just stopped in to ask You to help me out with a letter of recommendation for an apartment in that new luxury complex. I know I have the funds to make it happen, but funds are not enough to get you in. Basically, you need a recommendation from the elite of the elites. I couldn't think of anyone else to ask because I know they are all backstabbing, vengeful, self-centered, all eyes on me arrogant bastards! All they'll do is jump on the bandwagon, steal my idea, and weasel themselves into that very place that's supposed to be mine.

WHAT! What's that You say? How do I know the apartment is mine? Well duh, it has my name on it. Technically it doesn't, but let's keep that little secret between us. No one has to know. I just go around telling everyone apartment 3G is mine and they believe me. They have no other way of finding out. The building manager runs a tight ship. I tell You, they have some of the strictest policies I've ever seen! No one, and I mean no one is allowed in the building until they're assigned an apartment, and once in, they're sworn to secrecy. They're forbidden to mention who the other tenants are. Is that crazy or what? It sounds like some sort of secret society! Wait, am I signing my life away?

Oh my goodness, are You crying? If so, get a grip on Yourself! I thought by now You'd have put the hanky away and started to focus on getting me that letter. Come on, that's not too much to ask. You're not pulling the wool over my eyes. I've seen You do great and mighty

things. I've read about You doing great and mighty
things. By the way, why are You crying? I
thought crying is for babies? Toughen up! You're not a
wimp! So, what, they knocked down the church to build
that new complex. There are lots of churches and that one
was old. Pull Yourself together. For goodness' sake, are
You forgetting who You are? You're the head honcho,
the big kahuna, the man of the hour. You're the man who
rocks the world! Forget that, You're the creator of the
world! Wait a minute, what's that I see on the wall? Ah
yes, that award You won: The *Most Influential Person of
All Time*! What the heck! I don't recall seeing one of
those plaques on *my* wall. I wish I had that kind of power.

Self-Absorbed

GOD the Alpha and Omega

*[10] "The name of the LORD is a strong tower: the righteous runneth into it,
and is safe. [11] The rich man's wealth is his strong city, and as an high wall
in his own conceit. [12] Before destruction the heart of man is haughty, and
before honour is humility." ~ Proverbs 18:10-12*

Epistle No. 14

Dear GOD,

I'm getting ready to tell You something, You already know, but please just hear me out. I'm a psychologist, how could this be happening to me? I've been reassuring, coaching, analyzing, and guiding my patients for the past 15 years now and I can't even get my own life together. Where did I go wrong? I still find it hard to believe I'm in such a toxic relationship. I recall times she got upset because I didn't tell her how wonderful the meal was, and she became enraged. One night, she made my favorite, shrimp primavera and because I told her I had already eaten, she took the entire plate and threw it against the wall! GOD, it was horrible It was total insanity! There was shrimp, spaghetti, and marinara sauce splattered *all* over the kitchen wall. I never thought I would've been so frightened! Being a man and all, one would think I shouldn't have flinched. Well, guess what, I did more than flinch, I almost jumped out of my skin! LORD, to tell you the truth, I was terrified! I was in utter shock. Nevertheless, Father, even after all of that, I found myself comforting her. That was just the beginning of it all. Why didn't I just leave? The signs were there, but I thought she was just emotionally imbalanced.

GOD, please give me the strength to leave. I still love her, but I know this isn't healthy. It's just hard to leave because we have a son together. Even he's a target of her rage. I'm always walking on eggshells around her. I never know when she'll have a manic episode. She's a great person when she's – well, I don't know. I still haven't figured out what makes her snap.
I never know when she's going to have a psychotic break.

Lord, I'm both ashamed and afraid to call the police. The last time I called them, I ended up being the one hauled out of the house in handcuffs and jailed for 2 weeks! Yes, incarcerated for a whole two weeks, Lord! The police laughed at me and told me to man up! Then hauled me off to jail. I never felt so humiliated in my life! *I* was the abused and *I* was the one who called, but once they arrived, she cried crocodile tears and told them I ripped her shirt. Mind You, she ripped her shirt when I closed the door to keep her away from me. Her shirt got caught in the door and she yanked it out. But You already knew that. Did I forget to mention she's an expert liar? Well, I know You know the truth, even if no one else can see past her lies. Thank You GOD. I know it was You who convicted her. I know it was You who made her tell the truth in court. The only reason I was acquitted was because she finally admitted she was the one who attacked me!

I can't take it anymore GOD. The dish, the knife, a candlestick? Whatever's handy gets hurled at me. The throwing is crazy! My head's not a bullseye, although she seems to think it is. I'm tired of having to restrain her. I know her behavior is unacceptable, but what am I supposed to do? We have a child together. I know she'll end up getting custody. I'm afraid that if they give her custody, my baby will end up dead! I still have nightmares about the time she tried to throw our precious angel down the stairs. Even after all of that, I walked away from the argument. Maybe I'll just take my son and run!

I know GOD, I have to get myself out of this, but I can't do it alone. I need Your help. I'm tired of minimizing the situation. You know, living a lie, telling lies, and living in denial. I'm tired of feeling guilty, as if I'm the one to blame. I'm tired of feeling like I'm less of a man because I refuse to raise a hand to her despite *her* physical abuse. Lord, I'm just tired. I'm tired of being sick and tired!

Oh Lord, thank You for helping me realize and accept the fact that I'm in an abusive relationship and I'm being abused. Lord, I still need Your help. I need Your help now more than ever. I need You to give me courage. Lord, I won't be able to talk to anyone about this. LORD,

please help me get over my pride and the shame I feel.
Please give me strength Father. Give me the strength I
need to leave her. Give me the strength to move on.

Abused

GOD the Supporter

*[17] Recompense to no man evil for evil. Provide things honest in the sight of
all men. [18] If it be possible, as much as lieth in you, live peaceably with all
men. [19] Dearly beloved, avenge not yourselves, but rather give place unto
wrath: for it is written, Vengeance is mine; I will repay, saith the Lord." ~*

Romans 12:17-19

Epistle No. 15

Dear GOD,

Just *one* more high. If only I could get just one more high. *Oh* yeah, that very first high. My pain is gone, and my fear is no more, but I'm trembling. Why am I trembling? I can't stop shaking. Have mercy on me Lord. Have mercy on my soul. Oh Father, if only You would give me that one last high, I promise I'll make it my very last. No for real, this time I mean it. I've been saying that, but I haven't made any of them my last one. Oh, Father, I've failed You. Time and time again I've failed You. Oh my GOD, my precious Father, my Abba, I've failed You again!

Father, this time I promise, if You help me through the night, I'll only look to You for that natural high. It's just, the pain is so unbearable. I don't know how I'll make it through this. I swear this is gonna be the longest night ever! My whole-body hurts and I'm exhausted. I haven't slept in days. It feels like I haven't slept in ages. If only the deal hadn't gone bad. I'd have my money and my drugs. They robbed me! The pain has been excruciating! I haven't been able to sleep. The only thing that makes that pain go away is another high. I know I had no business being in that part of town, but I heard they had good stuff. A better fix, a better high they said and dumb old me believed them. It's like I have no fear when I'm high. Nothing seems to matter. Nothing *ever* matters, except getting high! Not even jail matters. Death doesn't matter. Disease doesn't matter. Cold, heat, thugs, bugs, none of those matters! Only the drugs matter! You have no inhibitions.

So here I am, with no money, no drugs, no high and almost no mind! GOD, I thank You. At least I'm not without my soul.

Stupid birds, would you stop singing! I'm trying to sleep! Wait a minute. Their chirping. The *birds,* the birds are chirping? The birds *are* chirping. Is it morning? Is it really morning? I can't believe it! I made it through the night. I'm alive! Can you believe it, I'm actually alive!
Oh my GOD, I made it through the night.

Addict

GOD the Healer

[3] "Thou shalt have no other gods before me. [4] Thou shalt not make unto thee any graven image, or any likeness of any thing that is in heaven above, or that is in the earth beneath, or that is in the water under the earth. [5] Thou shalt not bow down thyself to them, nor serve them: for I the LORD thy God am a jealous God, visiting

the iniquity of the fathers upon the children unto the third and fourth generation of them that hate me; ~ Exodus 20:3-5

Epistle No. 16

Dear GOD,

You told me to pray for the ones You instruct me to pray for. You told me to raise awareness about your Son. You told me to let as many people as possible know about what He endured. You've put Your child, a pastor, a husband, a father, my brother in Christ in my heart and my mind. You've assigned me this task.

GOD, my heart aches thinking of the injustice and cruelty my brother is facing. Imprisonment! Execution by hanging is his current fate simply because he refuses to denounce his Christian faith. Lord, how my heart aches. This is cruel. It's horrific!

Another brother decided to compile letters from fellow supporters to bring to him, his wife and 2 sons. I think it's a grand idea. Can You just imagine Lord, how alone he must be feeling? I've read he's been in solitary confinement for the past 2 years! They've also stated his health is deteriorating and he has been subjected to physical and mental abuse. He's the victim of *all* sorts of torture. GOD, I couldn't imagine being in his situation.

O.k. GOD, I'm gonna write this letter now and I need Your help. Help me write words of endearment. You know, words of encouragement. Father GOD, please help me write words You know will comfort him. Holy Spirit, please guide me while I write this letter. Thank You Father.

Greetings in the Mighty name of Our Most High and Almighty GOD, my brother. I am a supporter of you and your wife's efforts. Together, many Christians are standing in prayer for and with you. December 8th has been designated as a Global Day of Fasting and Praying on your behalf in hope that GOD will show you His favor, His mercy, and His grace.

May you find comfort in the Lord, knowing Our Lord and Savior Jesus Christ is forever with you. May GOD's angels surround you and GOD's oil running from the crown of your head to the soles of your feet. May you and your family be covered in the blood of Jesus of Nazareth.

My brother, stay the course knowing GOD's course is the only course that matters. May GOD continue to strengthen you in the darkest hours and may you experience GOD's perfect peace. May your soul dance with serenity and your mind remain on the heavenly. May your heart rejoice and your bones be limber. May you know that you never stand alone. My brother, you are loved from near and afar. You are not, have not, and will never be forgotten.

May your strength be renewed each day, as you meditate upon the sweet salvation of Our GOD. May your nights be days and your days be filled with joy, joy cometh in the morning. As your fleshly man walks this journey, know that countless angels of Our LORD and Savior walk alongside you. For the Spirit of the Most-High dwells by and inside you and the spirit of your brothers and sisters in Christ are moving in leaps and bounds to march beside you. As you stand for Christ, I stand with you. Let me reassure you, your matter is also my matter, and your burden is my burden. For the bible tells us we're our brother's keeper.

My brother, stay the course and be faithful until the end. For the one who redeems, and rewards is Our Father, the Most-High GOD Almighty! In Jesus' Holy and precious name, I pray for GOD's perfect will for you and your family.

Love, your sister in Christ Jesus of Nazareth,
Sophie

Well GOD, you've done it again! You never cease to amaze me. That's one of the most heartfelt and beautiful letters I have *ever* written, and I know it was all Your doing. Thank You Father.

Please have mercy on my brother tonight. Please give him Your peace. In Jesus' name I pray – Amen.

Sophie

55

GOD the Advisor

[2] "Bear ye one another's burdens, and so fulfil the law of Christ." ~

Galatians 6:2

Epistle No. 17

Dear GOD,

How'd he feel if one of his bastard friends did this to his mother?! How about if it were done to his daughter or his wife? How about his sister, his girlfriend, his grandmother, or any female he's close to? Oh yeah, I forgot, silly me, he doesn't respect women! He's just a bastard! I hate him! I hate him! I *hate* him! I know his mother must hate him too! She probably took one look at him and said, "I regret the day you were born!" It doesn't matter what she thinks anyway because he still did what he did.

My skin burns Lord, but I'm not getting out of this shower until I scrub everything off me. I can still smell his stench. Father, why did you let this happen to me? Why me Lord? What did I ever do to deserve this? All I ever did was do as You told me to do, love all people and treat others the way I want to be treated, but instead of me getting treated with love, instead of me being treated with respect, I got beat up, abused and taken advantage of!

Oh GOD, what if he has HIV. What if he has a disease? What if he gave me a disease? What if I'm pregnant? I can't have a baby – not his baby! Who's ever going to believe me? They'll treat me as if I'm the perpetrator, the accursed, the accused! I wasn't dressed in scanty clothes. I didn't flaunt myself in front of him. All I did was invite him over, after he said he needed to talk. He said he was going through major family issues. So, I let him in my house, and he violated me! This is what I get for trusting people. This is what I get for trying to help. I guess that's my reward.

Oh Lord, what am I supposed to do now? Who am I supposed to turn to? I can't tell my family. I don't want them to know. They're the last ones I want to know about this. I don't even want any of my friends to know. I don't need a pity party or anyone's sympathy! I just need this to go away! Lord, I just want all of this to go away. Lord, I *need* this to go away. Make it go away GOD. Please, just make it go away.

Sexually Assaulted

GOD the Consoler

[35] *"To me belongeth vengeance and recompence; their foot shall slide in due time: for the day of their calamity is at hand, and the things that shall come upon them make haste." ~ Deuteronomy 32:35*

Epistle No. 18

Dear GOD,

I'm really not sure how all of this praying stuff works, but here I am on my knees, giving it a shot. I've heard many people say, you have to pray on your knees. Some say I have to cover my head during prayer. Others have told me to be sure I anoint the crown of my head and the soles of my feet. Then some say I have to light a candle before I start praying. GOD, so many people have said so many things that if I told You about all of them, I would be here until Christ returns. Better yet, I think I would probably be here even longer than that. I mean, Jesus, Mary and Joseph, this whole praying thing has me spinning in circles. I'm so confused. I even forgot what I came to pray about. I'm just trying to make sure I get all the instructions down and then follow them. I'm exhausted just thinking about it.

Lord, all I want to do is pray. You know, talk to you. I want to build a strong relationship with You. I need to make sure I'm walking with You. I didn't realize that wanting that and obtaining it would be such a chore.

You know Lord, I just want to say thank you for helping me find my way. Thank you for never giving up on me. Thank you for sending Jesus Christ, Your only Son, to die for my sins. Lord, thank you for loving me. Thank you for always looking out for me even when I wasn't looking out for myself. Thank you for my family, the food on my table, the roof over my head, the clothes on my back, my health, my strength, and my job. Lord, I just want to pray for: sister Betty, sister Annabelle, Daisy, Ty, Odessa, and Suzanne. Oh, and I want to pray for brothers: Dan, Bruce, Wellington, Ivan, and Josiah. Lord, please watch over my family. Lord thank You, thank You, thank You for everything. Lord if I forgot to thank You for something, please forgive me. Hum, let's see, I think that's a sin. That's what one of the elders in my church told me. Oh yeah, and Lord, please forgive me if I have forgotten to pray for some people. I know *so* many people and they *all* need prayer, but I just don't have the energy to name them all. I don't even think I can name them all. I mean, I know for sure I would end up forgetting to include somebody. Lord, anything I forgot to do or say during my time alone with You, I ask that you please forgive me. Father, I repent of my sins. LORD, I'm new to this whole prayer thing and I just haven't gotten it all down pack yet. Amen.

Layman

GOD the Pleased

[14] "Ye are the light of the world. A city that is set on an hill cannot be hid.
[15] Neither do men light a candle, and put it under a bushel, but on a
candlestick; and it giveth light unto all that are in the house. [16] Let your light
so shine before men, that they may see your good works, and glorify your
Father which is in heaven." ~ Matthew 5:14–16

Epistle No. 19

Dear GOD,

Pwease watch over my mommy and daddy. They are a little too sweepy tonight to come and pway wit me. I think they forgot cause they fell asweep. GOD I guess you have to watch over yourself too because daddy said that I have a nodder daddy and dats you. So daddy, now you have a *lot* of work to do. I'm saw wee. Pwease don't be mad dat I made you have more work. I just want you to be safe too. Mommy said dat you always watch over me. She said that you don't wear pajamas. Mommy said dat you don't sweep. Mommy said you watch over everybody.

Jeezwas I pway for my brodder Quistofur. He needs a *lot* of your help cause he's alwayz pulling my hair and he's alwayz quwhing. I know you'll sabe him too. He doesn't mean it. He's just a baby. I think he quwhiez all da time because he don't like his quib. Maybe you can give him a nodder one. And Jeezwas if you kan't saw wee, den maybe you kan give me a nodder brodder kause Quistofur quwiez a lot.

Daddy, pwease let mommy and my odder daddy let me not go to skool. I don't like skool because mommy and daddy ahwent deer. Oh, and daddy, pwease let mommy and daddy send Quistopher to skool and not me. In Jeezwas name I pway. Amen.

Daddy I almost forget, you should qose your eyez and go to sweep now too. See I whamembah dat mommy said dat you don't sweep. Mommy said you don't where pajamas, but dats ok, you kan still go to sweep. GOD, you can take a nap because when I tell mommy I don't want to sweep, mommy says, "You're not sweeping, you're napping." Good night Jeezwas. I lub you.

Child

GOD the Touched

[13] "Then were there brought unto him little children, that he should put his hands on them, and pray: and the disciples rebuked them. [14] But Jesus said, Suffer little children, and forbid them not, to come unto me: for of such is the kingdom of heaven." ~ Matthew 19:13-14

Epistle No. 20

Dear GOD,

I think I'm ready to accept Jesus Christ of Nazareth as my Lord and Savior. Tell me what to do and I'll do it. You lead and I'll follow. I know all the Christians I've spoken to about this, told me it's simple. All I have to do is recite the 'Sinful Prayer' and then I'll have eternal salvation with You Lord.

O.K., so here goes:

Most Divine Father, please forgive me for my sins. I acknowledge that I am a sinner and that I have sinned against You. For that, I am truly sorry. I know my sins cause me to be separated from You. Please help me turn to You and away from my past sinful ways. Father, help me not to sin anymore. Lord, today I accept Jesus Christ as my Lord and Savior. I am asking Jesus to come into my life to rule and reign over me and everything I do from this day. I believe that Jesus Christ is Your only begotten Son and You sent Him here so that *all* sinners may have eternal salvation. I believe that Jesus died on the cross, was raised from the dead and is alive. I know Jesus hears my prayers. Father, I believe the Holy Trinity consists of

GOD the Father, GOD the Son, and GOD the Holy Spirit. Father GOD, please send Your Holy Spirit to help me do *Your* will. In Jesus' name I pray – Amen.

That's it?! Yippie! I'm saved! I'm saved! Oh my gosh y'all, I'm *so* saved! I just said the 'Sinful Prayer' y'all. It was that easy. It didn't hurt. I didn't have to do anything funky. All it did, was save me. Now I have eternal salvation. By the way guys, It's called the 'Sinner's Prayer', not the Sinful Prayer. Hehehe

Just Saved

GOD Rejoicing

"For God so loved the world, that he gave his only begotten Son, that whosoever believeth in him should not perish, but have everlasting life." ~
John:3-16

Epistle No. 21

Dear GOD,

You know I'm claustrophobic. Why didn't You give me a larger room? This place doesn't get good sunlight. You know what, this place doesn't get any light! Well, at least I can say this, the weather is great! The temperature is ideal year-round. I'm surrounded by water! What else could I ask for? Seriously, come to think of it, I got a really sweet deal. This was a really good find. You did a good job. For sure I'm gonna recommend You to everyone I know. In this economy, a realtor is a dime a dozen. They're scavenging around lurking in the oddest places just waiting and watching to see who they can reel in. I'm just counting my blessings. I'm glad You scouted me out and insisted I look into what You have to offer.

Well, isn't this just great! Just as I was thinking of all the positives about this place, the plumbing springs a leak! I have a major water pipe explosion going on here. Whadaya mean it's not that bad? Are you for real?! No, you didn't just say that to me. GOD, I have to worry about water damage! Hello . . .

Wow, this is just unbelievable. You've got to be kidding me. Some bozo is trying to move in! They claim it's my fault they have major water damage and that my lease is up anyway. They're acting as if I took an ax to the pipe and made all of this happen. I hear them saying, "For the past few months, I've made
my *neighbors* uncomfortable." *Excuse me*?! Not me. They said they've gotten complaints from my roommate that I'm constantly flushing the toilet and moving around, that she ends up being up most of the night. Can You believe that! They even said that all the greasy foods I enjoy, leave the place smelly, causing her to become nauseous! What an imbecile!

I'm not a drinker, but you don't hear me complaining when she drinks. I don't get offended; I just go to sleep. To be honest with You, I outgrew this place a little while ago. The clutter from my roommate was getting to be a bit too much. Nevertheless, I never complained to anyone. This is the first time I'm even mentioning my discomfort. She brings in all this junk into the apartment, hogging up all the space and forcing me to survive in a very tight space, but still, You never heard me say a thing. I just decided that maybe it's time for me to find a new place. I don't know, maybe I'm just being nitpicky. Truth be told, I think the real deal is, I've just outgrown this place.

So what do you say GOD, can You find me a bigger place? This time I think I want somewhere away from the water. Also, I think I'd like to live in a place that has all seasons. I think that might be nice for a while. Don't get me wrong or anything, I loved being surrounded by water and having ideal weather, but I think it's time for a change. Change is good yah know. Every once in a while, I think we just have to shake and bake and stir things up a bit. You know, be a bit of a pioneer, go conquer some new frontier, spread the wings. I think experiencing new things is vital. I think it'll be good for me. I think it'll be good for both of us.

You know GOD, I think I'm just gonna break out of this joint! What do I look like, a schmuck? I'm not gonna wait for them to come and pull me out of here kicking and screaming, unlike, my roomy. She's just gonna sit around and wait until they evict her and even then, she's not gonna leave. She's gonna wait until the sheriff comes, puts the metal to her skin, and yanks her butt out! What do You mean how do I know that? I know because she told me from the start. She's lazy! She sleeps all day. She said things for her are tight and if they ever try to put her out, they're gonna have to pull her out kicking and screaming. She said they're gonna have to pull her out feet first because she'll be hanging on to the pipes. I'm telling You, she's not gonna go without a fight! They'll have to haul her butt out of here. I tell You this, she's on her own. I'm outta here. I don't know about her, but I have integrity. Excuse me? The last time I checked, I was, and might I add, still am an upstanding human being. I deserve to be treated with dignity and respect! You know what, I'm not even taking any of this stuff with me. It was great while it lasted, but it's just gonna be extra baggage as soon as I step foot out the door. All this stuff is old, I'm just gonna buy everything new. They can put it all out with the trash. Come to think of it, it'll be nice to get a whole new wardrobe. A new environment and all the fringe benefits of living without a roommate. This is a good thing. Oh yeah, did I forget to mention that? Yeah, I think this time I'd be better off by myself. No roommates, no apartments, and no craziness. I think this time I'll go for a house.

Alright, I gotta get outta here. I have a headache. All this hustle and bustle around this place trying to make it to the front door is killing me. I mean look at this place. I have to climb over heaps and heaps of stuff! This chick is a hoarder. I have to squeeze through the hallway just to get out!

Listen, gimme a little push, will yah! I'm trying to maneuver through this mess! Push, push, I said push, not *pull*! Would you stop pulling on me! See what you did. You made me hurt my shoulder. Yeah, I know they were just helping. Yeah, I realize I'm out . . . duh, I can see that. Look, just give me a minute. After I got pulled

through all this junk, I gotta check and make sure I have all my body parts! Do You mind? After their barbaric pulling, I gotta make sure my whole body's still intact. Thank you *very* much! O.k. let's see – ten toes, ten fingers, um, my ears. Thank You very much!
Oh *GOD,* thank You. I'm breathing!

Neonate Twin

GOD Omnipotent

[5] *"Before I formed thee in the belly I knew thee; and before thou camest forth out of the womb I sanctified thee, and I ordained thee a prophet unto the nations." ~ Jeremiah 1:5*

Epistle No. 22

Dear GOD,

Huff – I can't really – huff – I can't really – I can't talk right now, huff, huff, huff. Oh GOD, if only You'll just help me run for 5 more minutes, I would be so happy. Yesterday was good. I did three hours on the treadmill, one on the elliptical, two on the bike, and 300 sit-ups. I lost count of all the laps in the pool, but I cycled *all* the way home. I spent most of the evening at the gym. I couldn't wait to get off work. I cycled to the gym and then jumped right into the aerobics class. I managed to eat a whole apple today which was only because I was forced. The girls on my job insisted that I go with them to lunch or else they would tell the boss I was late every day this week. Normally I'm punctual, but I just can't seem to get up in the mornings. I'm so beat when my alarm clock goes off, it's unreal. I end up rushing out of the house to put in some time at the gym before work. If only they would end that stupid step class 15 minutes early, I would make it to work on time. Maybe I'll just leave the class early. Oh my gosh, never! That's insane! I'm never ending any workout early. Absolutely not! There's no way I'm gonna miss my morning workout class. Do You realize how many calories I take in per day? ½ slice of bread with a slither of lettuce in the morning, a bite or two of fruit for lunch and then coffee the rest of the day. You'd be calling me Free Willy if I wasn't working out as much as I do.

You know GOD, I think it's time for me to switch my doctor. I went in all excited for my yearly annual, only to leave totally pissed off! Let me tell You the story and then tell me what You think. The audacity of my doctor to tell me I'm looking poorly. Pretty gauntly. He said I'm too thin! I asked him why he would say such a thing. I have been working out more than ever and watching my diet, yet I was still obese. He said that my body is covered in some sort of fine hair. I can't recall the fancy medical term he used. It was something like laguna, lasagna, la something. I said so what, big deal, I'm hairy. He said the type of hair that covers me is like peach fuzz, it's like what's on babies and that's not normal. Then he told me my electrolytes were all out of whack. He said the lab report was so bad, he's worried about me going into cardiac arrest. Cardiac arrest!? What?! I mean the only thing that was wrong with me was my foot. I had excruciating pain when I tried running on the treadmill. I told him that was the only thing wrong, and he said that's not odd for people like me. He told me I have a *stress fracture* and it's secondary to excessive running. *Whatever!* You don't have to be a doctor to know that. So, after that, I was given a list of negative things. I knew for sure that doctor man was just a negative man. I can't stomach negative people. I have to surround myself with positivity. You know, positive people, positive light, and positive energy. Do you know what I mean? Oh yeah, and listen to this, here's the doozie. Can you believe that after all of that, he had the nerve to hand me a piece of paper he called a referral. While I was glancing down at the paper, I heard him say, "I'm recommending you get a psychiatric evaluation. Dr. Liam is the best in the country, and he specializes in your sort of condition." What's that? No, I don't know what the diagnosis is! I don't know, because at that point, I tuned him out – *completely*. I decided I'm gonna get rid of him like a bad habit! What condition is this man talking about, I thought to myself. The nerve of him trying to tell me I'm crazy. What does pain in my foot have to do with me needing to get my head checked out? No, he didn't actually say that, but that's what he was implying. Only crazy people go to the psychiatrist. What does he think I am? Who does he think I am?! I'm no psych. I'm not some sort of crazy?!

O.k., o.k., I want You to take a look at me and then you tell me who's the crazy one. Look at my bum, it looks like a hippopotamus's behind. My arms are massive, and my boobs are like two watermelons stuck together. Oh yeah, let's not forget this belly. *Oh*, the belly. I have this hideous pot belly. It annoys the kat doodles out of me when everyone around me keeps telling me that I have a washboard stomach. What in heaven's name are they seeing? I have no idea. All my cousins keep saying they wish they could be as skinny as me, while I'm telling them that they need a psych eval and glasses for sure. Heck, they need to see my doctor because he's the writer of wacky referrals for wacky people.

The other day when I was walking to the subway, this scraggly looking man approached me and asked me if I model. My suspicion was confirmed, another deranged man. I looked at him like he had ten heads and stupid stamped on all ten of them! I politely replied – no. Next thing I knew, I was handed a business card that said, *Skinner's Modeling Agency.* No way he's an agent, I thought. He told me to give him a call and he'll make me a superstar. He said with a body like mine, I'll be in high demand, but they just have to work on my face. Work on my face, I thought. What's this man talking about, I'm gorgeous. Then I heard him say, "Pale-face, sunken eyes, sunken cheeks, and cracked lips just aren't sexy. Darling, you're looking a bit famished, very malnourished. No worries, we'll fix you right up. Call me," he said right before speeding off in his Porsche 911.

Well GOD, at least You love me just as I am. I love You too. I'm gonna forget about him. What does he know? It's not like he's a doctor or anything. See, I knew doctor man was a quack. Models are gorgeous!!

Anorexic

GOD the Sympathetic

"I beseech you therefore, brethren, by the mercies of God, that ye present your bodies a living sacrifice, holy, acceptable unto God, which is your reasonable service." ~ Romans 12:1

Epistle No. 23

Dear GOD,

The sun has fallen and now it will soon be dark. Along with the moon and the stars come the city lights, red, green, yellow, and white. They are the most amazing lights you'll ever see.

These city lights are like mothers. They shine so brightly never being afraid to show their true colors. When they shine, they do it with extreme care, but most of all they shine with pride. Proud to be the color they are and where they stand. They guide you home at night praying you'll walk a safe path. They are like your best friend. They warm your heart with love and they are your guiding light. Without them, we'd be lost in this place, a place not caring who we are, but what's in our pockets. Sometimes they give up on us and hide their feelings. When it rains and the weather is bad, they still shine *so* brightly. They'll make it through the roughest times knowing they want to give up, but yet, they gleam. Some of them give up by losing their light. They're the ones that aren't so bright. They ask for nothing much, only that you don't break them and that you give them a new bulb when their light has died.

Then you have the other lights. They're the ones that shine on the violence of the world. The criminals that haven't been found are known by our city lights. City lights are like people who mind their business. They see all, hear all and know all, but they won't say a word. They stand there and turn their faces the other way after all has been done; for they are the greatest witness of them all. City lights might be all that some people have. Think of the homeless, they have no one, but the city lights. They listen to them when they need someone to talk to and they keep their secrets to themselves.

City Lights, oh City Lights you are my dearest friend, therefore I have written this as a token of my love towards you. Maybe now other people will know why you mean so much to me. When I'm in a corner on the street you always keep me company. I'm happy when you let me know that you're there, but sometimes you make me angry. How could you leave me as soon as the sun comes up! Oh yes, I understand, you and the sun don't agree, for I am the less fortunate and you should think just a little bit more about me.

Homeless

GOD the Guiding Light

God is our refuge and strength, a very present help in trouble. ² "Therefore will not we fear, though the earth be removed, and though the mountains be carried into the midst of the sea; ³ Though the waters thereof roar and be troubled, though the mountains shake with the swelling thereof. Selah. ⁴ There is a river, the streams whereof shall make glad the city of God, the holy place of the tabernacles of the most High. ⁵ God is in the midst of her; she shall not be moved: God shall help her, and that right early. ⁶ The heathen raged, the kingdoms were moved: he uttered his voice, the earth melted. ⁷ The LORD of hosts is with us; the God of Jacob is our refuge.

Selah."

Psalm 46:1-7

Epistle No. 24

Dear GOD,

You're the only one who can hear me. No one else cares. They don't talk to me, and they definitely don't share things with me. They act as if I am not here. I'm invisible to all of them. Why do they want me around? Why am I even around? What's the sense? All I do is sit in this same spot all the time.

No one has ever taught me how to do a thing! I don't even know what smells so good. Is it something I'll put into my tummy? I hope so because my stomach hurts. I feel like I am going to just die.

I wonder if someone's home? I wet my pants. Oh no, this is horrible! It doesn't feel good. Now I'm not going to smell that sweet smell anymore and my bottom is going to start hurting again if they don't do something fast.

Stop it! Who's that touching me? Why are they pulling my head? What are they messing around with up there? Every time it's the same thing. They pull and they prod and they poke and then it gets worse.

That's cold! Stop it! See, that's what I was talking about, this thing is all over my body. Wow, it smells good, and my wet underpants are gone. Everything else on me is gone too. Will someone get me out of here, I can recall thinking.

Finally, she's here, I remember saying to myself. What's this touching me, I thought to myself. It's hard on one side, but soft and prickly on the other. Big on top, small on the bottom? Stop it! Why is she pulling my hand? What is she doing with the middle of my hand? What's that – B-r-u-s-h my teacher wrote in my hand with her finger. Ok, why is she moving my head and pulling my hair? She's just like the others. There she goes again with that doodling – H-e-a-d, H-a-i-r, H-a-i-r-b-r-u-s-h – then the prickly thing was on my head again. My teacher wrote b-r-u-s-h-i-n-g h-a-i-r. Next, I felt that cool thing, and my teacher wrote w-a-t-e-r. She put water all over me.

Well, I can tell you this, that day was a bit frightening. My excitement and eagerness to figure things out didn't stop me from being terrified. On that day, I learned many words. The ones I can recall are GOD, communicate, speak, hand, writing, water, cool, soul, brush, hair, hairbrush, bathe, clean, creation, create, love, grace, care, help, beautiful, perfect, smart, blind, see, deaf, hear, mute, speak, human and being. It was on that day I learned I'm a beautiful human being. I learned it's important for me to bathe and brush my hair and that my teacher was there to help care for me. My teacher used to say, "Cool water helps to soothe the soul." I learned that being blind, deaf, and mute won't stop me from becoming learned. I learned I have to communicate by hand and later I will be able to speak. I learned I don't have to remain mute. On that day, I learned, despite all these disadvantages, GOD loves me. I know He created me, and I am *His* perfect creation. On that day, I learned of GOD's, grace.

Conquered Disability

GOD the Gracious

"And as Jesus passed by, he saw a man which was blind from his birth. ² And his disciples asked him, saying, Master, who did sin, this man, or his parents, that he was born blind? ³ Jesus answered, Neither hath this man sinned, nor his parents: but that the works of God should be made manifest in him." ~ John 9:1-3

Epistle No. 25

Dear GOD,

What am I supposed to give the kids for dinner tonight? It's only 4 pm, but they'll be home soon, and I know they'll be saying, "Mom what's for dinner." I know for sure they'll be asking because *I'm* already hungry. What am I supposed to do? I only have about $2 to my name and Lord you know, that's not even enough to pay attention. I know, I'll call my friend. I hate to have to call because he can never seem to get it right. Every time I've asked for money, he's always late getting it together. He always promises me and low and behold, I'm left waiting. Well, right about now I don't have much of a choice. Everyone I know is struggling. We're just in hard times and everyone is feeling the heat.

Good news Lord, He called and offered to order food for me. I must say, I was a little shocked. I usually have to ask. Well, thank you GOD! I'll order pizza. That's the cheapest and can share for more people. Ok, I better call and order before the kids get home.

GOD, can you believe the card payment was declined?! I knew it was too good to be true! What am I supposed to do now? He said he knows he has enough on the card. Well, let's just say he only had $20 bucks in his account. The whole order was $40 after delivery. Lord, I don't know what I'm going to do. Another night with us going to bed hungry isn't good. Father, I'm just thankful we have a roof over our heads. Guess it's another night of plain white rice. Lord, please don't think I'm complaining because I'm not, I'm grateful.

Knock, knock, knock. Who could that be, I was thinking?

"Pizza delivery," I heard the stranger say.

Pizza? I didn't order pizza. Hello... sir? I didn't order pizza.

"Yes miss, this *is* 55 Montcler Ave. isn't it? I have a delivery for 2 large pies, garlic knots, and a 2-liter soda."

"No, I think you made a mistake. When I called to order I asked the man to check the card first to see if it would go through and he said it didn't go through. So, I don't understand why you're here."

"Just a minute, let me call the store. Ma'am, the boss said you're supposed to pay cash."

"I don't have cash. That's why I asked him to check before processing anything. He knows the card was declined so why did he put it through? I don't have the cash to pay. Let me speak to your manager please."

"Here you go, his name is Joey."

"Hi, Joey."

"Hi."

"Listen, you weren't supposed to deliver this. The card didn't go through, and I don't have the cash to pay. Fine, I'll keep it. It's ok, no worries. Mistakes happen, even the best of us. You won't lose, I'll pay you before the night's out."

Lord, of course You know I was panicking about how I would pay. Joey didn't ask me to pay – he told me to keep the order because it was his mistake, but I felt bad. I didn't want him to take a loss or maybe even lose his job. Times are hard and jobs are even harder to come by. We all make mistakes You know. On top of me feeling bad, I was also so embarrassed when I noticed my neighbors were standing outside and heard everything. Yes, that's right GOD, You guessed it, they heard when I said the card was declined and I had no cash to pay. Ugh! Talk about a major catastrophe. I don't think I could have felt any lower than I was already feeling. Nevertheless, I took the pizzas, soda, and knots into the house, and then I called my friend. Can you believe Lord, he said he has to go put money on his card! Excuse me?! What does he mean he has to put money on the card? Didn't he know that! Oh . . . I get it, you can order and receive things with wishful thinking – NOT!

Next thing I know, the phone rang, and it was, Mr. *Never Keep His Word* on the other end telling me to go ahead and buy the food now. I tell You Lord; I didn't let on that the food was delivered already. So, I called in, paid Joey, and all was well. I know it was a gift from You Father because it's not as if I swindled someone out of their money. I never told them to deliver *anything* because I didn't place an order. Joey said he forgot to clear the order off the computer, the chef processed it, and the delivery guy delivered it. Thank You GOD for being the perfect choreographer. Thank You GOD for the opportunity to receive free food, but most of all GOD, thank You for being You!

Blessed

GOD the Choreographer

"And it shall come to pass, if thou shalt hearken diligently unto the voice of the LORD thy God, to observe and to do all his commandments which I command thee this day, that the LORD thy God will set thee on high above all nations of the earth:

[2] And all these blessings shall come on thee, and overtake thee, if thou shalt hearken unto the voice of the LORD thy God. [3] Blessed shalt thou be in the city, and blessed shalt thou be in the field. ~ Deuteronomy 28:1-3

Epistle No. 26

Dear GOD,

Why have you chosen me? I always prayed and expressed my love and gratitude to You without any expectations. In my most prolific moments in prayer, I came to realize that Your magnificence, Your power, You're just being You, is incomprehensible. I would sit so still on the pier gazing upon the endless horizon, using the keenest eyes to evaluate that point at which the ocean meets the sky. I hoped to see a separation or a distinguishing point, possibly a line of demarcation, but in all attempts I was unsuccessful. Having exhausted all of my sincerest attempts to demystify the mystic, I finally settled down and concluded that this too is a miracle of GOD. How still the water remained each time my soul was at ease was more than amazing to me. Quite baffling at times, it was if I must say so myself. How even the brainless sea obeys Your very will. Never would the sea move past *that* predestined point. How could one deny You? How could one deny Your very existence, I often thought to myself? This is a question that plagued me each time I sat by the seaside. What an awesome GOD we serve, I thought. My GOD, my GOD how excellent is thy name in all the land! What a Mighty GOD we serve.

On the nights when the moon was high and at its fullest, the waters raged and roared with a controlled subtlety. I'd watch in awe of its midnight temperament. I wonder how can there be people who doubt Your power? How could there be people who doubt Your existence? How could there be people who doubt You at all?!

So, Lord, I have this alphabet soup of letters after my name and yet I haven't been able to make good use of the soup. I wonder Lord, what are You up to? Although I don't know Your plans, I am certain there is no diabolical affiliation with Your master design. That, I am certain of. Still, I wonder why am I here? I've been stagnant for quite some time now and Lord I won't lie, it's been frustrating. I blame the devil and say he's a no-good son of a gun, but then I wonder. I wonder if this stagnation is some sort of benefit. I know that sounds strange, but really, when I think about it, this could be a period of rest.

I was always on the run; going to school full time and then scurrying off to work. I barely had time to think. My nights were occupied by homework and fatigue. Huh, I tell you, I wonder. Then off to medical school during the day and graduate school at night as I worked on a dual degree. Well of course during that time I couldn't work, but I tell you the workload was like five full-time jobs!

Then once again, my nights were filled with studies. Oddly enough, it was doable, and it became second nature to me. Never thought I would say that, but hey, the truth will set me free. I looked forward to the day when I would have a normal schedule, but instead, I went from a schedule of 'the maniac kind' to 'no schedule' at all. Well Lord, if that's not a doozy for yah then I don't know what is. Well, of course, it's not a doozy for you, but it's sure a doozy for me.

Lord, I wonder, is this a type of sabbatical? Hum, I'm curious. It felt good at first but then that feeling became stale real fast. No work, no money, no vision of the future, no anything. That can't be good. A life without a vision is a dead life. The good thing about it is, I didn't say – no hope. Thank goodness because hope deferred makes the heart sick and hopelessness paves the way for death! So, I suppose I'm not doing too bad after all.

The beating of stagnation has left me a little tethered. It may seem as if I'm not that vivacious visionary as once before, but never fear Lord, I'm still standing. I'm still standing strong on a mountain of hope. My hope is in You Lord and no one else. I wonder what great things you have in store for me. I wonder.

Lord I know it's through You that all things are made possible and it's through You, all things are done.

Oh Lord, You *are* my GOD and I will exalt
You. You *are* my GOD, and I will praise You. "I will
praise You, O Lord, with all my heart: I will tell of all
your wonders." ~ <u>Psalms 9:1</u>.   In Christ Jesus of
Nazareth's name I pray – Amen.

Wondering Sophie

GOD the Omnipresent

> [5] *"If any of you lack wisdom, let him ask of God, that giveth to all men liberally, and upbraideth not; and it shall be given him."* ~ *James :1-5*

Epistle No. 27

Dear GOD,

I'm 75 years old and looking for a job. I can't afford to live decently off the state's salary and my pension, so I have no choice other than to find a job. Lord, it's rough. I pray for those who are unemployed. The market has been devastated for quite some time now and many are seeking employment. Each time I do a job inquiry, I get those weird stares, You know, the ones like, "You're too old." I've even had some people outright tell me that to my face. It saddens me and many days I lose heart, but then I see, and I am reminded the people in my age range are finding work.

Father, I've managed to save a little, but when one of the kids need help, those funds start dwindling. Lord, thank goodness I can still take reasonable care of myself. Thank You GOD for that. Father, I hope I never see the day when I have to use a stairlift, shower and toilet rails, or a powered scooter. Lord, I must say I am very thankful for the good health You have given me. You have been so merciful to me. Most of my friends are suffering from arthritis, dementia, rheumatism, or one of those plaguing ailments people of my age often get. So far, my only physical issue is I'm not hearing or seeing as well as I used too. I'm not complaining though, dear Lord, because I can still hear, and I can still see! I know it could be worse.

Lord, I think You'll be proud to know I've released a lot of those fears I used to talk about. My honey's been home with You for 10 years, 3 months, and 5 days as of today, and no I haven't gotten over it, but I have learned to cope with it. Oh Lord, I sure do miss my darling. I know my beloved is in good hands and soon I will be too.

Lord, remember that abandonment issue I often discussed with You – well let's just say that's no longer an issue. I have good news Lord; the kids are moving back to the neighborhood. They agreed they should all be closer to me. So, see Lord, I no longer have to worry about being alone. They should be arriving by this weekend. I can't wait! I get to see my babies, my grandbabies, and my great grandbabies! Oh, thank You, Lord.

Lord, I'll be honest with You; I do have some regrets. You know those things I did and said in the past – they still weigh heavily on my mind. I know I can't undo those things. I think I've lived long enough to at least know that much, but Lord, that still doesn't stop me from wishing I could change things. I always thought I'd be

living a plush retired kind of life. I thought I would be in the class my friends call, the WOOPies
– **W**ell **O**ff **O**lder **P**eople, but I suppose that wasn't my fate. I'm more than happy with the group I'm in. We call ourselves the POOW's – **P**eople **O**f **O**bvious **W**ealth. Yes Lord, I think everyone would agree, at my age with my health and strength, I am wealthy beyond belief.

Elderly

GOD the Sustainer of Life

"The thief cometh not, but for to steal, and to kill, and to destroy: I am come that they might have life, and that they might have it more abundantly." ~
John 10:10

Epistle No. 28

Dear GOD,

Oh my goodness, if only I could get a minute to myself. Why does everyone have to run to me for every little thing! So what if I'm in charge! I know I'm in charge! What do you think, I'm stupid?! I'm not a moron you know. All I'm asking for is just a few minutes to settle in when I get to the office. I'm not a robot for heaven's sake! Yeah, yeah, yeah, they can take the big bucks and stuff it, cause frankly, I'm just tired of all of this! You know, I really think it's time for me to retire. I've been doing this long enough now. I think I've earned a well-deserved break.

Day in, day out, I face the same humdrum. You know, the same nonsense, different day. I only wanted this position because I thought I'd be able to make a change. Now I see, change here is virtually impossible. The board members are always hovering over me each second of the day, asking me this, asking me that, telling me this, telling me that. Well sure, that's fine and dandy when it's done in moderation, but come on, the nagging and controlling are completely unnecessary. I know how to do my job and I just want to be left alone to do it! I cancel my order of micromanagement!

I took this company from ground zero to the empire it is today. No other CEO has been able to do that! I'm the reason why the company is a 100-billion-dollar business. Forget about the charitable contributions that were given. Those contributions were based on *my* upstanding relationship with all the donors. *I've* managed to sign on 80% more investors than any other CEO here. Our stocks have risen tremendously despite the failing economy and our company surpassed all other US-based companies when it comes to employee retention. As far as I'm concerned, I've gone above and beyond my call of duty. You don't have to take my word for it, the proof is in the pudding. The next time you pass by a Newsstand, pick up this month's issue of Forbes Magazine. Guess who's featured on the front cover? You've got it, badda boom badda bang, none other than Your one and only – Mwah!

O.k. so if we're finished here, I'll have to excuse myself. I hate to be a prude and rush off, but I have a string of meetings lined up for today. As a matter of fact, my next meeting is in 5 minutes!

Boss

GOD the Chief

"Let every soul be subject unto the higher powers. For there is no power but of God: the powers that be are ordained of God." ~ Romans 13:1

Epistle No. 29

Dear GOD,

If I'm caught, I'll be delivered to my country's wicked ruler and his totalitarian regime. Despite the crippling fear, Lord I've decided to speak out against their brutality. You've allowed me to escape and find refuge and for that, I am so grateful. This new sense of freedom has empowered me more than my fellow countrymen, so, I must not offer them a disservice. Father, with the little power I have, I must view this as the greatest power *anyone* can possess. I'm no longer powerless as I was just a few days ago. Father, I will use this power to expose the grief and torture my countrymen have been facing, and I will continue to face as long as they remain under our country's ruler. I will use this power to help those who are powerless.

GOD, tonight I have written a letter to the Refugee Society to be posted first thing in the morning. It is my hope they won't just add my letter to their countless stacks of letters from others like myself. I know my efforts will not be a waste of time because they have given and restored hope to many refugees who have cried out in desperation. You, oh Lord, have made this possible. Like the many others, they will investigate the heinous crimes I have written about in the letter. They will step in to assure my people receive justice and freedom.

GOD, although I'm shivering with fear of what will happen to me and my family if I'm ever caught, I feel compelled to carry on. The life I lived in my country was no life at all. Neither is my family exempt from such a hopeless life. GOD, I am more fearful of what they will do to my family if I am caught, than what torment, torture, and some of the most unspeakable acts I may endure.

Lord, I pray to You tonight to have mercy on me, but more so please protect and have mercy on my family and my village. Watch over them and protect them because only You know how much danger they're in. If help doesn't arrive in my village for them before I am discovered missing, I'm afraid they will meet their demise. As retaliation for my escape, they will be raped and beaten, while many, if not all, will be executed. This is the fate many members of the village will face. The government knows that when one goes missing, they can only do so with the help of the others. But Father, they know wrong. They never stop to think that one might have been killed by the lions. They are too evil to think in such a way. They automatically assume that a member has escaped and has planned to betray the country. Anyone who escapes the clutches of their iron fist does so only by You, Father, who made it possible.

Father, I beg You please spare my village. If You don't Lord, then my village will be torched. The mere thought of this makes me weak. This nightmare plagues me night and day, awake or asleep. Father, I pray for asylum in my new home and I'm pleading with You on behalf of *all* other asylum seekers from my country. I plead with You for their safety and their freedom. My faith resides in You oh GOD. You are the great *I Am,* and nothing is impossible nor possible outside of Your will. I pray in Jesus Christ of Nazareth's name, Amen.

Refugee

GOD the Sovereign

[18] "He doth execute the judgment of the fatherless and widow, and loveth the stranger, in giving him food and raiment. [19] Love ye therefore the stranger: for ye were strangers in the land of Egypt." ~ Deuteronmy 10:18-19

Epistle No. 30

Dear GOD,

Tonight I decided to use my downtime to talk with You. I am so grateful for You LORD. I was very sick and in a lot of pain for the past 3 days. I thought I was going to die! I ended up resorting to the very pain medications I *swore* I'd try to avoid, but Lord, I just couldn't. The pain was so unbearable that even with medication, I still felt terrible! The medicine took the edge off the pain with the first dose, but it took about 3 doses before I was totally relieved.

I told the doctor that medicine makes me sleepy. The medicine just knocks me out! I mean, I am comatose within no time. It's like a horse tranquilizer hit me! When I take the medication, I literally pass out, not having a clue when it hits me. That's pretty pathetic if I must say so myself. Lord, I just end up slobbering all over the place and feel like I am drowning. I know, I know, pretty gross and probably too much information, but hey, it is what it is. I must admit though, it is the best sleep I get whenever I take the meds. I sleep like an angel! O.k., I didn't mean to get sidetracked. Back to my issue. My doctor said the medicine I'm on doesn't cause drowsiness. She said there's no way it should cause drowsiness. Well, I ended up checking with a pharmacist who said it *can* cause drowsiness even though it's not common. I don't know Lord if the medication knocks me out or if it's because I'm usually in so much pain that by the time the medicine kicks in, I'm so fatigued, I end up passing out. Hum, I wonder. Well, that's neither here nor there. All I know is I'm finally able to settle down and it sure does feel good. Thank GOD for modern science.

Hey Lord, wait a minute, I just realized something I don't have an issue! I'm o.k. Thank You, Lord, for that. I was just stopping by to say, tonight, I *am* tired. I'm beat! Zonked! Kitt and caboodle. I've just had it! I can't even keep my eyes open. I gotta get some shut-eye or maybe not shut-eye, but just stay in the bed, watching t.v., praying to drift off into never-never land.

Lord, I love You. Thank You Lord for loving me for just who I am. Sweet Lord, I thank You Lord for loving me. You're the source of my life, You're the Lord of my life, You're the One I adore. I truly adore You. I thank You Lord for loving me for just who I am. I love You, Lord. Good night and Amen.

Chronic Pain

GOD the Reliever

[16] *"For which cause we faint not; but though our outward man perish, yet the inward man is renewed day by day.* [17] *For our light affliction, which is but*

for a moment, worketh for us a far more exceeding and eternal weight of glory; [18] While we look not at the things which are seen, but at the things which are not seen: for the things which are seen are temporal; but the things which are not seen are eternal."

~ 2 Corinthians 4:16-18

Epistle No. 31

Dear GOD,

It's another year and so far, nothing. Last year was very depressing and although I was hopeful, nothing major manifested. Things got worse in my opinion. I prayed, and I prayed, but still nothing. Where are all those wonderful things You promised me Lord? I've been faithful! I've been diligent in keeping up with my communication with You. I know, I'm not perfect nor will I ever be, but Lord I sure do try. Sometimes it's hard to stay on the right path, especially when things seem to be going down the tubes faster than gravity pulls on a thing. The offers that come my way that all seem to be the best thing since sliced bread are all so very tempting. Lord, how much longer will I be able to resist the wiles of the devil? How much longer will I have the strength to say no to *all* the unethical opportunities that come my way?

Listen Lord, I'm not gonna lie to You; sometimes my mind sways towards the vial and negative. Sometimes I lose myself in the moment and I wonder, where are You GOD? I wonder; why You haven't helped me. I wonder, why You haven't provided a way of escape for me! The wicked prospers and You don't see *them* begging for bread while those who are faithful and loyal to You seem to have the worst lives. With sickness, poverty, and mockery playing a major role in our lives, why would anyone want to become a Christian? Our lives seem so dismal, and poverty seems to be such a close friend that so many people tend to say they don't want to be a Christian. They say they'd rather live how they are living because they are not suffering. Well Lord, all I have to say is, it's pretty hard to convince them to walk on the straight and narrow when they see me and so many other so-called "Christians" living in poverty.

Hey Lord listen, I'm not trying to be disrespectful or anything, well You know my every thought anyway, I'm just being real. GOD, when will you vindicate me? When will you come and anoint me with all the desires of my heart? When will You make it so I won't be the laughing stock of the crowd!

Hopeful

GOD of Peace

[8] "For he that soweth to his flesh shall of the flesh reap corruption; but he that soweth to the Spirit shall of the Spirit reap life everlasting. [9] And let us not be weary in well doing: for in due season we shall reap, if we faint not. [10] As we have therefore opportunity, let us do good unto all men, especially unto them who are of the household of faith." ~ Galatians 6:8 -10

Epistle No. 32

Dear GOD,

I know this is gonna sound crazy, but Lord, why did You make me this way? I'm so skinny it's unreal! I look at all the women walking around saying they just wish they could lose weight and I think to myself, what in the world is wrong with them? I'm afraid to even say anything to them because You know, you should love yourself. I know they're just going to scuff at me. They always say it's easy for me to say things like that because I have the perfect body. To me Lord, I am just a train wreck! I'm as skinny as a rail and each time the wind blows, I feel like it's gonna knock me down. When I go shopping, I can barely find anything nice. My boobs are so flat that sometimes I wonder if I'm really a man! And let's not talk about my rump! Well, that's just a story in itself. If I sit too long, my backside hurts. Obviously, there just isn't enough cushion. Then sometimes, when I'm in bed, my side hurts. My bones are torturing me!

GOD this is insane! What the heck's really going on here? No matter how much I eat, I just can't seem to gain weight! I eat everything in sight, and still, nothing! Nada, zip, zero! I do all the don'ts and still no hope. I eat late at night, go to sleep, and still, I'm as skinny as a rail! I eat all *types* of fatty foods, barely exercise, and still, nothing. I have to buy those pushup bras and padded panties just to look like a young teenage girl. Even with that, sometimes a baby has more fat than me! I'm serious! For heaven's sake GOD, why will I look like a teenage girl after all that padding when I'm supposed to be grown and sexy? The women go crazy over my shape and some men just can't get enough, but *I* just absolutely hate it! Lord, I want the curves. I want the D cup. Better yet, I want the DD cup and I'm willing to trade places! I want the Coca-Cola bottle shape. I think it's so attractive. Lord, I want to be a voluptuous woman. I'd trade places with anyone of them any time of the day.

Skinny

GOD the Friend

[14] "I will praise thee; for I am fearfully and wonderfully made: marvellous are thy works; and that my soul knoweth right well." ~ Psalm 139:1-4

Epistle No. 33

Dear GOD,

Who am I to trust? This is a heavy burden, and I never knew I'd have such a struggle. Father, I am the constant target of the devil himself! I feel like I'm a bullseye for his practice. I knew that struggles would ensue, but I didn't imagine a burden as such. I am the constant target of criticism from my congregation and even my family. If I try to take time off to relax, everyone becomes a critic. It's as if I'm supposed to be superman. Father, only You know my woes and foes, my inward parts.

GOD, how am I supposed to juggle my ministry, personal, and professional family life? If I give it to the ministry, my family becomes disgruntled. If I give to family, social, and personal, my congregants become disgruntled. Father, what am I to do? If I seek wise counsel, I become leery of who to trust. Lord, it's so lonely at the top. I know Father that you've said, "To whom much is given, much is required." I suppose this is the requirement. I suppose this is my fate. Father, does it really have to be so?

Father, not only do I have to deal with my problems, but I have to deal with and anticipate the problems of those you've entrusted into my care. How do I figure out future problems Father? You're help and guidance are my lifeline. Lord, surely, I would perish without Your hand upon me.

Forgive me Father. I sometimes become impatient when I try to anticipate the future problems of Your sheep. This impatience I know Father is a sin. Therefore, I repent before You my GOD. Father, I try my ever best not to offend Your children. It is not my intention to grieve the Holy Spirit. I know that would be displeasing to You and consequences would ensue. Therefore, I meditate on Your Word which says, *"But whoso shall offend one of these little ones which believe in me, it were better for him that a millstone were hanged about his neck, and that he were drowned in the depth of the sea."* ~ <u>Matthew18:6</u>   In doing so, I remain in proper order.

Father, I know You have entrusted me with Your precious children and I am responsible for their souls. I know I must win souls to Christ of Nazareth and not be harsh or unapproachable in my demeanor. When I'm attacked by some, they often say to me, "What makes *you* so great? What makes *you* any different from me?" The best and only response I give GOD is, "The difference between you and I is, I *was* a sinner, who's now been saved by GOD's grace and you *are* a sinner, who has not been saved by grace. Would you like to take this opportunity to give your life to Christ?" Father, I don't know if this is harsh, but I think it's ok. I must say, Lord, I have managed to win many souls to Christ after saying this. Maybe, for some reason, they are so eager to close the imaginary gap they think stands between us and, as such, they eagerly jump at the opportunity to have what I have. I'm not sure what it is Father, but what I'm sure of is that souls are being won to Your Son. Whatever it is that happens when I say those magical words, it's winning souls to You my Lord. My Father, I thank You for Your blessings. It is the Holy Spirit who convicts. I merely speak, which is nothing in comparison to the Holy Spirit because Lord, in times past, You've used even a *donkey* to speak.

I pray Father, that You will help me not stumble and You will keep me on the righteous path. I thank You Father for sending Your only begotten Son Jesus Christ who died so that all who believe in Him will have eternal salvation. Strengthen my faith and keep me pure in Your sight oh Lord. Thank You for sending the fire of the Holy Spirit to purge my sinful ways and thank You for always protecting me. Thank You for covering me in the blood of Jesus. In Jesus' name I pray – Amen.

Bishop

GOD the LORD

"A bishop then must be blameless, the husband of one wife, vigilant, sober, of good behaviour, given to hospitality, apt to teach;." ~ 1 Timothy 3:2

[18] *"If the world hate you, ye know that it hated me before it hated you.* [19] *If ye were of the world, the world would love his own: but because ye are not of the world, but I have chosen you out of the world, therefore the world hateth you.* [20] *Remember the word that I said unto you, The servant is not greater than his lord. If they have persecuted me, they will also persecute you; if they have kept my saying, they will keep yours also.* [21] *But all these things will they do unto you for my name's sake, because they know not him that sent me.* [22] *If I had not come and spoken unto them, they had not had sin: but now they have no cloak for their sin.* [23] *He that hateth me hateth my Father also." ~*

John 15 18:23

Epistle No. 34

Dear GOD,

No matter what I do I just can't seem to get this weight off! I've tried and tried and have failed each time! Lord, I have prayed and prayed and prayed until I think I have prayed my brains out and still nothing! Lord, why do I have to struggle with this? Why do I have to be a fat slob! Yeah, I know You're saying that I shouldn't be so hard on myself, but no matter what I do, this weight has pledged allegiance to me to never leave nor forsake me!

The doctor says I have an irregular acting thyroid gland and that it's not an uncommon thing. He said it's because my thyroid is sluggish, that's why I'm having difficulty losing weight. Ok, whatever! Try telling that to the people who walk by me gawking because I'm so obese. Lord, You should see the looks on their faces as they see me coming; pure disgust! I'm like the wretched old dirty bum! Well, Lord, I tell You at this point, I think even the bum gets more respect than me. How dare them! They have the audacity! They don't even know me. They don't know anything about me or my situation. All they do is snicker and pass hurtful remarks about *why* I am so fat.

I'm not lazy Lord and I do want to exercise, but sometimes I'm just so tired. I'm always short of breath it seems like and it's just the worst feeling ever! Then when I do muster up the strength to go and become proactive, I have the whole world staring at me. I remember one time I was running, but it was a slow run. It was so slow that had I been going any slower, I would've been stopped! Anyhow, there I was, feeling good about myself, that I started to make a change. You know, I was being really positive when this obnoxious muscle head on the beach yelled out, in front of everyone, "Move it fatty! Move it, move it, move it!" GOD – really?! And some say Satan ain't real? Huh, go figure! I just saw him in the flesh! I remember being so embarrassed, it was unreal. After that day, I started to get up before the roosters crowed and went to do my run. It felt good and Lord it gave me time to talk to You. That was our alone time, and I was never happier. Come to think of it Lord, every time I talk to You, I feel better. I started out praying bitterly and now I'm smiling. I realized all the good that has come out of having my condition. Yeah, I know GOD, I'm not skinny, but thank GOD I'm not the marshmallow man! Best of all, I have a relationship with You and that's something I never had before.

GOD, I love You and thank You for being You. You are my Father. You are my best friend. You are my everything now and even when this all comes to an end. In Christ of Nazareth's name, I pray. Amen.

Obese

GOD the Mind Changer

[19] *"What? know ye not that your body is the temple of the Holy Ghost which is in you, which ye have of God, and ye are not your own? [20] For ye are bought with a price: therefore glorify God in your body, and in your spirit, which are God's."*

~ 1 Corinthians 6:19-20

Epistle No. 35

Dear GOD,

Oh Father, what have I done to cause You to forsake me? I've served You with all my mind, with all my soul, and with all my heart. I never asked for anything much and I always work to win souls to Christ. I've been a faithful servant Father. I know my sins are all before thee, but Father, I repent every day. I am but a mere mortal and my eyes and heart sometimes give in to the wicked ways of this world. It's not something I'm proud of nor will I ever be, but Lord, I know You are forever with me.

Father, You have blessed me abundantly. For this, I thank and honor You. You are the great I Am, the maker and master of all things. You are my El Shaddai, my Jehovah Rapha, my everything. So Lord, why have you forsaken me? You took my one and only son from me! Every Sunday I get up and I preach to Your people, the sheep of Your flock in attempts to steer them the right way. Every Sunday I preach the true and living Gospel. I thought this would be pleasing to You. Instead of watching over me and my boy, you took my son from me. I raised my boy in the church, teaching him how to love, honor, and reverence You. He loved You *so* much LORD, he made sure he was the first person in church before service to get the sound and lighting going. This was his faithful service to You Father until that one Sunday morning. GOD, why didn't You stop him from being electrocuted? Why didn't You send Your angels to watch over him? He was doing *Your* work, for the glory of *Your* Kingdom. Lord, it was right under the stage where I stand to minister to the people that he breathed his last breath. Father, how could this be? How could this be right?! Every Sunday I dread going to minister because old memories arise in my mind. Father, how am I supposed to go on? How do I convince the people You *are* a fair, loving, and trustworthy GOD when they look and see the torment my soul is encountering? How do I move on? Father, how can I move on? Oh Father, help me! Help me please Father, help me.

Pastor

GOD the Father

⁺ *"Blessed are they that mourn: for they shall be comforted." ~ Matthew 5:4*

Epistle No. 36

Dear GOD,

Auntie said to pray to You, and You will answer and guide me through anything. I'm scared again GOD. Today I have to walk to school and those gangs are out in front of my house. I can't tell my ma because that wouldn't make me a man. I can't tell my paw because he's gonna tell me to toughen up. GOD, you know I don't wanna join a gang, but they always pressure You into being 'down' with them. All my boys and all their girls are down with them because they're scared, they're gonna kill them. GOD, I'm the last one on the block to convert and GOD I'm fighting like mad to do the right thing. GOD, I've seen my boys' moms cry because they lost their son. GOD, I don't want to see my ma or paw cry over my bloodshed. I don't want to take nobody's life either. I'm not into hurting people. GOD, I don't want to be caught up in the drug thing.

GOD, my boy told me to try this drink and it was cool, but truth be told GOD, I didn't like it at all. I had to be cool, so I played cool. I told them it was alright. I lied! GOD so far, the only thing that's saving me is the fact they know I'm not scared to brawl. I rather have peace, but in my hood, you have to fight for your rights. They lay off of me because I'm the one who looks out for everyone. I'm a *cool* cat. I tell them I'm not down with all the stuff they're doing, and they listen, but Lord for how long will they listen? Lord for some reason, I couldn't stop them from joining the gang.

GOD, one day I think they may gang up on me and try to force me to join. GOD, I'm afraid. I'm afraid GOD, that if I don't join, one day their minds will change, and they may just pump me full of bullets.

GOD, auntie always says to pray to You and ask You to cover me in the blood of Jesus. She said this will save and protect me from any harm. So GOD, here goes – GOD as I walk to school I'm asking that You cover me in the blood of Jesus Christ of Nazareth. Protect me Lord because I can't do it on my own. Much love – Amen.

Teenager

GOD the Delighted

[2] *"God is jealous, and the* LORD *revengeth; the* LORD *revengeth, and is furious; the* LORD *will take vengeance on his adversaries, and he reserveth wrath for his enemies.* [3] *The* LORD *is slow to anger, and great in power, and will not at all acquit the wicked: the* LORD *hath his way in the whirlwind and in the storm, and the clouds are the dust of his feet.* [4] *He rebuketh the sea, and maketh it dry, and drieth up all the rivers: Bashan languisheth, and Carmel, and the flower of Lebanon languisheth.* [5] *The mountains quake at him, and the hills melt, and the earth is burned at his presence, yea, the world, and all that dwell therein.* [6] *Who can stand before his indignation? and who can abide in the fierceness of his anger? his fury is poured out like fire, and the rocks are thrown down by him.* [7] *The* LORD *is good, a strong hold in the day of trouble; and he knoweth them that trust in him."* ~
Nahum 1:2-7*

Epistle No. 37

Dear GOD,

Well, it's a new year again. Lord, this year feels different. I'm usually so depressed around the holidays, but this year things are different. I don't know what it is and I can't quite put my finger on it, but what I know is, it's something good. Something good is gonna happen to me.

GOD, each year I put my hope and my trust in You. Each year, I profess this year is going to be the year. A year of prosperity, a year of great things, a year when I get myself back on track.

For the past few years, I have been lost. I have felt so displaced I wondered why I wasn't erased. It seems like such a waste to be here if I'm not being productive in Your sight. I think we're all too be busy going about our work, but Lord, unfortunately, some of us, well most of us, become consumed with our projects. We lose sight of the real reason why we're here. Many of us seek our ambitions instead of Yours. I don't know GOD, maybe that's what happened to me. Maybe that's why I'm in this rut. Whatever it is, boy oh boy Lord, I tell yah, it isn't good. Ok, well let me say, that it doesn't feel good.

I know You know all, see all, and do all things, but Lord why do I suffer so much! I hate to say this because it seems selfish since there are so many others who are suffering in the most horrific ways. GOD, I know, every man thinks his burden is the heaviest. I know this is the furthest thing from the truth. If you gave one person more than the other, that would mean You're an unfair GOD and I know You're not! No matter how I feel, what I think, or even what I say sometimes, I know inside and out You *are* the true and living GOD. You are the only One who can make all things possible. No matter how bad I think things are here, it could always be worse. Father, You know all I say to myself is that even if I have to live a life of maybe 80 or 90 or even 100 years here in distress, it will all be worth it for an eternity of the sweet salvation I've been promised in heaven with You. GOD, I know one day it will all come to an end and that's the day I look forward to. There is no better gift for me than to know eventually I will spend eternity with You. Just to sit by Your feet and watch time go by is such a sweet thought.

GOD, You *are* my everything! Just the thought of You brings me bliss. Some may say I'm living in a fantasy world and yes, they may even be right, but it's ok. I'm ok with my fantasy. Heaven's not my present reality, but sooner than later by Your grace, it will be. It will be as long as You – Father – continue to have mercy on me.

Keep me from doing that which is offensive to You Abba. Send Your Holy Spirit to minister to my heart and keep me of sound mind and body. Prevent the wickedness of the world from consuming me and transform me into a soul in which You will be pleased. Father God, please watch over me. Have mercy on me and please forgive me for all my sins. Whatever I have done, will do or am doing to offend You, Father, I beg Your pardon Your forgiveness. Forgive me, for I am mere mortal. You made me. Have mercy on me and guide me in the way in which You want me to go. You are the potter, and I am the clay. I am ready to be molded to Your ways. In Jesus Christ mighty name I pray – Amen.

Humble

GOD the Gentle

[12] "I know both how to be abased, and I know how to abound: every where and in all things I am instructed both to be full and to be hungry, both to abound and to suffer need." ~ Philippians 4:12

[6] "But he giveth more grace. Wherefore he saith, God resisteth the proud, but giveth grace unto the humble." ~ James 4:6

Epistle No. 38

Dear GOD,

I'm the mother and the father to my kids. I didn't plan for this to happen this way. Don't get me wrong Father, I love my kids with my whole heart and my whole mind, but Father, sometimes it just gets so hard. I never have a minute to myself. Sometimes I just want to breathe. I mean, I know I am breathing, but it sure doesn't feel like it. I've exhausted family members *and* friends in asking them to babysit. No one wants to watch babies on the weekends, especially when they have their own. Yeah, it's cute, and it's ok the first two or three times, but after that, it becomes burdensome. The whole thing gets scary real fast.

GOD, You know my job is really stressful and they don't even pay me enough! Nevertheless, I'm not complaining. I'm thankful. Father You've provided me with a job and steady income. No, I can't always buy my babies the things they want, but I've always been able to buy them the things they need.

GOD, I really need You to step in and be a father to my kids. I know I say I'm the mother and the father, but GOD, truly I can't be a father to my boys. I don't know the first thing about being a man. You made me a woman.

One of the boys has special needs and GOD, I tell You, the cost of health care is astronomical! His care has drained me financially, physically, and emotionally. How can I be a good mom to my boys if I'm exhausted all the time? Oh GOD, what I would do just to get a good night's sleep.

Lord, please help me. I feel like I'm drowning. Sometimes I feel like I'm suffocating. I go from work to home to school to the kitchen. I go from preparing dinner to homework, to bath and then bedtime. Lord, I have no time for myself. I know You're probably tired of seeing me crying myself to sleep every night, but Father, I don't know what else to do. It just hurts so bad. When I'm in bed, I'm all alone. What I wouldn't do for the comfort of a man. A companion, a stable relationship is what I need Lord. Not just any man, but a good man, a husband. Father, please send me a man who can and will be a good father to my boys. I need a man who will be a good husband to me. You know GOD, a man who knows how to be a man. GOD, who am I kidding? Who wants a woman with so many kids? No one wants all this responsibility. Who's ever going to want me? Who is going to be so considerate and compassionate to want to marry a woman like me? They'll probably come along, want to have a good time, and then they'll be on their way. I may not know who will want me, but one thing I know for sure is, thank GOD, I'll always have You.

Single Parent

GOD the Head of the House

> [25] *"I have been young, and now am old; yet have I not seen the righteous forsaken, nor his seed begging bread." ~ Psalm 37:25*

Epistle No. 39

Dear GOD,

So this is what it feels like to be married. I never thought I'd see the day this would happen. Me, married. Oh GOD, I'm so happy! I hope this feeling never goes away. I hope this feeling lasts forever. I feel like nothing will ever go wrong. Oh my, I believe I'm in love. I'm in love! This is heaven on earth. I just know You made us for each other. I've waited patiently, ok maybe not patiently, but I did wait in faith. I waited for the day You would send me my one true love. They're right when they say it is better to have loved and lost than to never have loved at all. I'm not anticipating losing my love, but Lord, if I did, I could honestly say I would never trade this feeling for anything in the world.

Today we start our life together. Today we are husband and wife. How amazing is that! GOD, I'm still pinching myself. I can't believe this is real. It's all so surreal. I could just lie here in bed all day! Today, the air smells fresher and is crisper than the day's past. The birds are chirping louder and longer. The sun's rays kiss my skin.

Lord, I can't stop smiling. I never thought I'd see this day. I had faith in You GOD. However, at times, I did have those days where I became worried. It just seemed like I was destined to be a loner. My ethics likes and dislikes always seemed to be so farfetched from everyone else where I began thinking I would end up alone. GOD, I tell You, I still held on to my faith. In the back of my mind, I had faith You would surprise me with the ultimate surprise one day. I always reserved space in my mind and my heart for the promises you promised all who are faithful and trust in You. Yes, my faith did waver, and no I'm not proud to admit that, but my faith never left completely. I had my ups and downs, but even when I was down, I managed to dangle on that string of faith. I had faith the size of a mustard seed.

Oh my GOD, thank You. You're so good to me. Jesus, You're my Savior, You're so good to me. Ha! I think that's a hymn in a famous Christian song! GOD, this is truly a match made in heaven.

Newlywed

GOD the Match Maker

[18] *"And the LORD God said, It is not good that the man should be alone; I will make him an help meet for him."*

[24] *Therefore shall a man leave his father and his mother, and shall cleave unto his wife: and they shall be one flesh.* [25] *And they were both naked, the man and his wife, and were not ashamed."* ~ Genesis 2:18, 24-25

Epistle No. 40

Dear GOD,

Today is Baby's first day home. We couldn't be any prouder than we are right now. We could hardly wait to get baby into the house. The nursery is so beautiful. We painted it yellow because we weren't sure if we were having a baby boy or girl. We just prayed to have a healthy baby and now we have exactly what we prayed for. Our sweet bundle of joy has finally arrived. Each time I hold our precious angel, I can't stop crying. Ten toes, ten fingers, eyelashes to die for, and the sweetest angelic smile ever! That smile graces my baby's face. I know GOD, all mommy's and daddy's think their bundle of joy is the most beautiful, but Lord I know for sure my bundle of joy is a flawless angel!

All our selfish ways have gone out of the window. Ever since we knew we were expecting, all the things we shopped for were things for Baby. We're both shopaholics and we both know how to do some damage in the stores, but this time around, it was all about Baby and we didn't even think twice. Everything we did was centered around our angel. Our car and home have been baby proofed and we've changed our schedule to assure we can accommodate baby. All vacations are off! Well at least until we can figure out how to take our angel and still have a safe and fun time.

GOD, I would've never thought I would be changed! I would have never thought *we* would've been changed. I feel *so* special and thankful You've decided to bless us with our healthy bundle of joy. GOD, our angel is our pride and joy. Thank You GOD for our angel kissed, and GOD blessed baby. I couldn't have asked for anything more.

First Time Parent

GOD the Multiplier

[27] "So God created man in his own image, in the image of God created he him; male and female created he them. [28] And God blessed them, and God said unto them, Be fruitful, and multiply, and replenish the earth, and subdue it: and have dominion over the fish of the sea, and over the fowl of the air, and over every living thing that moveth upon the earth." ~ Genesis

1:27-28

Epistle No. 41

Dear GOD,

I hate all the things of this world that are in place to keep people in bondage. All I own I have because of me! I have everything I want because I have worked for it! I don't take from society without giving. I give back and I'm not a leech to society. My company employs thousands of people. I give people an opportunity and a way to take care of themselves. I give them the fishing rod and teach them how to fish. My success is attributed to me and no one or nothing else!

I've built a perfect world for myself. Within my world exist all I need and all I want. I even share what I have with others without them having to ask me. I'm a good person. I help others and I'm kind to all. I don't care what anyone thinks. I'm a self-made billionaire and I'm doing just fine on my own.

Hold on a second here, wait a minute, who am I even talking to? In my world, You, whoever You are, don't even exist!

Unbeliever

GOD the Patient

[36] *"Therefore let all the house of Israel know assuredly, that God hath made the same Jesus, whom ye have crucified, both Lord and Christ.* [37] *Now when they heard this, they were pricked in their heart, and said unto Peter and to the rest of the apostles, Men and brethren, what shall we do?* [38] *Then Peter said unto them, Repent, and be baptized every one of you in the name of Jesus Christ for the remission of sins, and ye shall receive the gift of the Holy Ghost.* [39] *For the promise is unto you, and to your children, and to all that are afar off, even as many as the* LORD *our God shall call." ~ Acts 2:36-39*

Epistle No. 42

Dear GOD,

I was so depressed. The girl I was dating broke up with me. I knew that night was going to be my last night. I planned on killing myself. I had a gun! It was fully loaded and ready to go, but then there was a knock on the door. My buddy from work – who happens to be a Christian – came by to see if I wanted to go to a service at his church. I didn't feel like going anywhere, but I did promise him we'd hang out this week. So I went to his church service which was ram-packed! They played a movie and music afterward and then the pastor stood up and ministered. For some strange reason, every word he said, I swear, it applied to me! I was flabbergasted, but I sat and listened. At that moment, he ministered to my heart and suddenly, it seemed as if everything was better. The pastor offered everyone who wanted to receive Jesus Christ, to come up to the altar and give their life to Christ. At that moment, I stood up and made the decision to give my life to You Lord. It was on that day my life began. It was on that same day; I almost took my life. That day ended up being the day Jesus saved my life and because He saved my life, decision to give Him my life.

Thank You GOD for Your mercy and grace. If it weren't for You Lord, I would have been dead.

Saved

GOD the Savior

"And you hath he quickened, who were dead in trespasses and sins; [2] Wherein in time past ye walked according to the course of this world, according to the prince of the power of the air, the spirit that now worketh in the children of disobedience: [3] Among whom also we all had our conversation in times past in the lusts of our flesh, fulfilling the desires of the flesh and of the mind; and were by nature the children of wrath, even as others. [4] But God, who is rich in mercy, for his great love wherewith he loved us, [5] Even when we were dead in sins, hath quickened us together with Christ, (by grace ye are saved;) [6] And hath raised us up together, and made us sit together in heavenly places in Christ Jesus: [7] That in the ages to come he might shew the exceeding riches of his grace in his kindness toward us through Christ Jesus. [8] For by grace are ye saved through faith; and that not of yourselves: it is the gift of God: [9] Not of works, lest any man should boast. [10] For we are his workmanship, created in Christ Jesus unto good works, which God hath before ordained that we should walk in them. [11] Wherefore remember, that ye being in time past Gentiles in the flesh, who are called Uncircumcision by that which is called the Circumcision in the flesh made by hands; [12] That at that time ye were without Christ, being aliens from the commonwealth of Israel, and strangers from the covenants of promise, having no hope, and without God in the world: [13] But now in Christ Jesus ye who sometimes were far off are made nigh by the blood of Christ. [14] For he is our peace, who hath made both one, and hath broken down the middle wall of partition between us; [15] Having abolished in his flesh the enmity, even the law of commandments contained in ordinances; for to make in himself of twain one new man, so making peace; [16] And that he might reconcile both unto God in one body by the cross, having slain the enmity thereby: [17] And came and preached peace to you which were afar off, and to them that were nigh. [18] For through him we both have access by one Spirit unto the Father. [19] Now therefore ye are no more strangers and foreigners, but fellow citizens with the saints, and of the household of God; [20] And are built upon the foundation of the apostles and prophets, Jesus Christ himself being the chief corner stone; [21] In whom all the building fitly framed together groweth unto an holy temple in the Lord: [22] In whom ye also are builded together for an habitation of God through the Spirit."~ Ephesians 2:1-22

Epistle No. 43

Dear GOD,

I know I've sinned against You. I've lied, cheated, and mislead the government of my country. Father, I beg You, please have mercy on me and forgive me for my sins. My country oppresses the people, and they don't give any of the regular people a chance to survive and make a good living. We're all basically living in poverty. My husband works and so do I, but still, we can barely afford to feed our children. In my country, people have to pay for their children to go to school, so if I want my kids to receive an education, we have to come up with a lot of money. Father, I make an honest living, but it's not enough for us to give our children a brighter future. We're not wealthy people and we don't have anything to pass down to our children. We live from hand to mouth, day to day. Father, I'm afraid that this life we live will one day be the fate of our children.

Father, I know there is better, and I know You want and have better for us. Father, You said, there's no good thing that You will withhold from me. I've prayed, and my husband has prayed, and we have sought Your voice. Father, I'm not sure if this was the way we were to go, but this was the only way we saw possible. We decided to run away to the land of the free. We paid a lot of money to get documents to come here. Lord, You know those documents are not legit. They were just a means for us to get to where we needed to go.

Every day I worry if they'll catch up to us and send us back to our country. Oh Father, I pray faithfully that You will watch over us and have mercy on us. I know I shouldn't be praying for You to bless such a deceitful act, but Father, this was the only way we knew how to provide a better life for our children. In this country Father, we have the opportunity to succeed. The harder we work; the better chance we have for success. Back home in our country, it didn't matter how hard you worked, you'd never make it anywhere. Our government's an oppressive government. They live to torture and torment the poor citizens of the land, but it's not like that here Father.

We've been here for one year now and so far, we have managed to open a little coffee shop. We even bought a single-family home although we have five kids, and all our children are going to some of the best schools for free! Father, I know it's because of Your blessings. The money we're making helped us apply for legal citizenship, which should be all squared away hopefully within a year. We've met good people who helped us open our shop and maneuver the system and for that, I am so thankful to You GOD. I thank You for everything You have given us and all You continue to do for us.

Father, thank You so very much for loving me and my family. Thank You for loving us! You love us so very much; You've allowed us to achieve the best. I thank You for our business, our home, our health, and the safe passage that we took when being smuggled here. Thank You, Father, for Your favor and Your grace. In Jesus' name I pray – Amen. By the way Father, why do they call us aliens? I know that should be the least of my worries, but that's something that really bothers me.

Illegal Alien

GOD the Way Maker

⁹ Thus speaketh the LORD of hosts, saying, Execute true judgment, and shew mercy and compassions every man to his brother: ¹⁰ And oppress not the widow, nor the fatherless, the stranger, nor the poor; and let none of you imagine evil against his brother in your heart." ~ Zechariah 7:9-10

Epistle No. 44
Dear GOD,

I'm ready to come home now. I've served You *all* my life. I hope I've done a good job. I know I've fallen short of Your glory, and I ask You to forgive me Father. I served You the best way I knew how, and I just pray that my efforts were pleasing to You, but now GOD I'm ready to come home. My bones are old, and I think my duty here is done. I've raised my family to love and honor You and GOD thank You for keeping them on the right track. For once in my life, I feel comfortable saying, "I'm ready." Many times, before I knew I still had work to do, I pleaded with You for more time and more time is what You gave me. Lord, You are so gracious. Thank You GOD.

I've seen many sunrises and sunsets and now I'm ready to see eternity with You Father. I've prepared my family for my departure the best way I know how and Lord, I think they're ready. I'm at ease and I think they are all at ease too. If they're not, then Father, they sure are doing a great job playing it off. Honestly Lord, I do think they are ready. I've made it my business to teach them from an early age that death is to be celebrated, not dreaded. They know that if they're born again, which they all are, then their eternity is sealed in the heavens with You, my GOD. So, GOD, they all know this is a time to celebrate. They know that my spirit will be free, and I will be at total peace. Father, I know now, I am ready. I am ready to go when You're ready to have me. You have blessed me abundantly and I've had the good fortune of living a wonderful life. Pitfalls, pit stops, and just pits overall were no stranger to me, just as You weren't either. Because I knew You *all* along, I managed to weather the storm, but more importantly, it's because You watched over me why I managed to weather the storm.

GOD, thank You for giving me a wonderful life. You gave me a life I wouldn't trade with anyone for anything. Amen.

Dying

GOD the Receiver

"The LORD is my shepherd; I shall not want. ²He maketh me to lie down in green pastures: he leadeth me beside the still waters. ³He restoreth my soul: he leadeth me in the paths of righteousness for his name's sake. ⁴Yea, though I walk through the valley of the shadow of death, I will fear no evil: for thou art with me; thy rod and thy staff they comfort me. ⁵Thou preparest a table before me in the presence of mine enemies: thou anointest my head with oil; my cup runneth over. ⁶Surely goodness and mercy shall follow me all the days of my life: and I will dwell in the house of the LORD forever." ~ Psalm 24

Epistle No. 45
Dear GOD,

Today is a good day. I have good days and bad days. I hate those bad days. It just seems like I can't shake that negative feeling when I wake up in the morning. Although I'm getting better at shaking it. Lord, I know through Your Word I can choose the thoughts I have. Sometimes bizarre things pop up in my mind, but then I chase them away with Your Word.

I'm still single Lord, but today *is* a good day. I've decided to look at today as another day of golden opportunity. I've decided to take full advantage of each day I'm single. I still would like to become physically fit, so today is another day I have to enhance my workout and training. I would also like to learn how to make exotic dishes. No GOD, nothing crazy or slimy or – well You know – nothing that will make me gag, but those dishes that are palatable and foreign to me. Also, I think I need to work on my relationship with You Father. I mean, it's pretty stable now and I think we're doing ok, but ok really isn't good enough. I need fantastic! Superb! I need phenomenal! So I think this is a good time for me to strengthen my walk with You.

Lord, You know I have those trying times. So, I suppose I'm not quite ready as yet for my ideal mate. Oh yeah and I almost forgot, I need to work on my attitude. My level of patience seems to be dwindling as I age and that for sure isn't good. It's unacceptable on every level. GOD, You know I'm a work in progress. Go ahead, just slap that sign back on me, *Under Construction.* No worries Lord, I'm not upset. I know I'm a diamond in the rough. I know You're refining me, so when my honey comes along I won't and can't get passed by. I'll be as shiny as gold.

Thank You Lord. I love You.

Single and Waiting

GOD the Partner

[11] *"For I know the thoughts that I think toward you, saith the LORD, thoughts of peace, and not of evil, to give you an expected end. [12] Then shall ye call upon me, and ye shall go and pray unto me, and I will hearken unto you. [13] And ye shall seek me, and find me, when ye shall search for me with all your heart." ~ Jeremiah 29:11-13*

Epistle No. 46

Dear GOD,

I know my people are superior and that's a fact! It's our duty to educate and tame those of the other races. My parents and grandparents can't all be wrong in their teaching. They all taught me and my sister that we are the elite. They said we're the chosen ones and we should never forget that. They said mixing with others from different races will only contaminate and weaken our superior race. They told us and demonstrated to us that people of the other kind don't care how you treat them. They don't treat themselves good and they definitely don't treat the people in their race well. They all squabble, fight and kill one another over the silliest of things. They speak in a strange language, something they made up randomly. They're ignorant! They call themselves by the worst names. I mean seriously derogatory names and it makes them happy. But meanwhile, if we, the elite, use those same names towards them, they become irate. What kind of people are they?! They're morons! Ignoramuses, if you ask me. Well, it is true, I shouldn't be as harsh in judgment. I and the people of my race are civilized. We know better. We don't get upset over their behavior because we understand they don't know better. They can't help themselves. They are to be pitied because their brains are smaller than ours.

They are a beast of the worst kind and this is how they are to be treated. They like ill-treatment. If we speak kind and proper words to them, they become baffled and bewildered. They stand and make crude jokes about our etiquette and how we speak. Our proper way of speaking is grounds for their comedy. They're so simple that when one of their own kind attempts to adopt *our* ways and style of speaking, they ridicule *them* and ostracize them. They might as well banish them from their community because that person no longer feels welcome in their town. How crude are these people? I don't even think they should be given the title people since they act like savages. I think another name would best suit them.

Even the bible tells us we are the original people, You know. We are the first. We are the elite. GOD, I can recall my grandparents saying, "We are the embodiment of civilization. These people are not to be feared, but instead are to be contained, controlled, and dominated because if they are not, they will infect those of *our* superior race.

We are to use any means necessary to control the rate at which they reproduce and advance within our society. Friendships are to be limited and conversations are to be kept at a minimum. Your children are not to become friendly with *their* children and the adults are not to mate with *their* adults. This is strictly verboten. They are a contaminated species, and they are a

plague to society. The world would be better off without them, but GOD, You know best. Our loving GOD knew exactly what He was doing when He created them. They were put here to serve us and to be at our beck and call. They are our footstools."

So GOD, till this day, I hold fast to the teaching of my ancestors. I am obedient to Your Word. Your good Word says, "Honor thy father and thy mother that thy days may be long upon the land which the Lord thy GOD giveth thee." That there Lord is in the fifth commandment. Yes sir, I know my commandments! Yes Lord, my good and faithful GOD, You have blessed me with 103 wonderful years thus far and I pray You will give me a few more. The only complaint I have is I sometimes get a little confused. These people of the lesser race seem to know more than I initially thought. Ever since I've been in the hospital all the caretakers have been from the inferior race and they seem to be keeping people alive. I'm not dead yet and after they treated me, I did feel much better. I told them not to touch me, but they laughed at me, called me senile, and proceeded to treat me. I'm not as strong as I used to be so I'm not able to fend them off. They end up having their way with me. *I'm not senile*, but

I am frail. I am weak and feeble. Who am I going to complain to Lord; I have no family that comes to visit me. The only one who comes to visit me is the colored girl who comes and reads to me every day. Sometimes I say things to her, and she gets upset, but I can't seem to figure out why. Nevertheless, she continues to visit me, and she continues reading to me. LORD, I must admit, I do like the colored girl. I reckon she's grown on me. I think some would say I'm pretty fond of her.

Racist

GOD the Pruner

[22] *"Ye shall not afflict any widow, or fatherless child.* [23] *If thou afflict them in any wise, and they cry at all unto me, I will surely hear their cry;* [24] *And my wrath shall wax hot, and I will kill you with the sword; and your wives shall be widows, and your children fatherless." ~ Genesis 1:27*

Epistle No. 47

Dear GOD,

I'm married, I'm a minister of Your Word, yet I still struggle. Lord, You know me. You've known me since the time I was formed in my mother's womb. You know me better than I know myself. Lord, why do I struggle with fidelity! No matter how hard I try, I can't seem to shake this urge. It's as if I just can't be satisfied when I am with my wife. She does a good job and I love her, but I find myself looking at other women and even wanting to be with other women. I don't know GOD, but for some reason, I find it takes more than one woman to satisfy me. I'm not normal Lord, because surely, this isn't normal. Father, I pray You take this insatiable desire out of me.

Father forgive me, I have sinned. I am as filthy rags standing before You. Each day I lie to my wife telling her I'm going one place when I know that I am heading to the other woman's house for a few hours of pleasure. I try to shake this urge and get rid of my habit, but Lord so far, I have failed.

A friend asked me two questions that got me to thinking and really analyzing my ways. She is the only person who has ever been able to cause me to truly evaluate myself. I mean GOD, no matter how many pastors or bishops or men and women of GOD I've talked to, none of them have ever been able to reach down into my soul and turn me inside out. I know You are the One who sent her to minister to me. I was convicted on this one day when I told her that I just can't stop doing what I'm doing. I confessed my sins to her, and she asked me why I won't stop. I told her I just can't! After extensive counseling with her, she hit me with the question that woke me up. She said to me, "If you were to die today, where do you think you would spend eternity; heaven or hell?" I responded by saying hell. Then she said to me, "If you stood before GOD today and He said to you, 'son, explain your life to me and why you are doing what you're doing now,' what would you say?" At that point, I was dumbfounded. I gasped, hung my head low, and said, "I wouldn't be able to explain myself to GOD. I would be ashamed." Then she said to me, "So are you ok with that? Are you ok with being ashamed in front of GOD?" "No," I said! It was on that day I reevaluated my life and realized the seriousness of my situation. It was on that day I witnessed with great depth of the Holy Spirit's conviction.

Cheater

GOD the Seer

[27] *"Depart from evil, and do good; and dwell for evermore." ~Psalm 37:27*

[16] *"Confess your faults one to another, and pray one for another, that ye may be healed. The effectual fervent prayer of a righteous man availeth much." ~ James 5:16*

Epistle No. 48

Dear GOD,

I don't profess to be without fault, but I know You're pleased with many of my ways. I am a pillar in my community because I adhere closely to your laws. I hold fast to always displaying the highest level of integrity. Each day I strive to live by what I know will be pleasing to You and in so doing, You have blessed me abundantly.

Lord, I confess my sin before You. I know You teach us not to fear, but Lord I *am* worried about my children. Even though I teach them to worship You and to always give You the praise, I'm afraid they're not doing as I raised them to do. So, GOD, please accept my prayer on their behalf. Allow me to atone for *their* sins.

Father, I don't know what else to do. I have asked for pardon for my children, and I have served You the best way I knew how. Yet, this is my fate. In one-day Father, I lost it all. The firemen said they had never seen a house go up in such a quick blaze. They couldn't have done anything. Nothing was salvageable. Lord, I didn't care about my wealth, but I did care about my wife and kids. My wife, my daughter and my son were all taken from me in an instant.

Father, all I know how to do is to praise You. My business, my home, and all my loved ones are gone. Not even the support of my friends can I rely on. They all sit and criticize me. They're supposed to comfort me, but instead, they snicker, whisper, and tell tales about me to each other. Not one of them has stood up for me much less consoled me.

Lord, why was I even born? To live a life like what I had and then have it all taken away from me just doesn't make any sense. I know Father that You give, and You take away, but Father why? Even the friends You have sent to be a shoulder to cry on are all critics of me and my situation. They aren't making me feel any better. GOD, despite my feelings, I'll still pray for them. They need prayer. I know their actions are not pleasing to You. They kick and abuse me while I'm down. It's ok Lord because You *are* the restorer, comforter, and healer of all. Father, forgive them and have mercy on them. Watch over them and keep them oh Lord. In Jesus' mighty name I pray – Amen.

Upstanding

GOD the Blesser

[15] "Though he slay me, yet will I trust in him: but I will maintain mine own ways before him. [16] He also shall be my salvation: for an hypocrite shall not come before him." ~ Job 13:15-16

[23] "The steps of a good man are ordered by the LORD: and he delighteth in his way." ~ Psalm 37:23

Epistle No. 49

Dear GOD,

I thought by now I'd be stronger than this. Today marks the first anniversary since I've lost my darling. I've been grieving for the past seven years, and I'm still stuck in a rut. I'm tired of being tired – of grieving, but I can't seem to shake this feeling.

When we received the terminal diagnosis six years ago, each day thereafter was as if I was walking on eggshells. I just never knew when our time together would come to an end, but Lord, I thank You. My love's terminal diagnosis gave us time to say goodbye. It gave us time to prepare, although I don't think anyone is ever prepared to let go. Lord, thank You for giving us that time – it was needed.

Oddly enough, we managed to mix in fear with love, joy, denial, bargaining, anger, appreciation, and grief. We spent six years in fearful anticipation of that soon to come, but an unwelcomed dreadful day. Lord, I'm still living that way. Each day I fear what the future has in store for me. I fear I will end up alone. What if I never find another love to share my passion with? What if our rhythm is off? I fear I will never meet another love who will complete me. I fear to be alone. Lord, my pain has multiplied, and my fear has escalated. My partner is gone. The love of my life is gone for good.

The emptiness and stillness I feel when I sit alone in our home are sometimes so unbearable. The house feels like winter – all year around. It seems as if summer never arrives, and spring goes and hides. Some days are better than others. I cry a little and I cry a lot; it just depends on the day. When memories hit me in the face, I cry buckets full, and days when the memories slowly appear, I cry a little less. I struggle something awful with mixed emotions. Why do I feel guilty when I cry less? I think I feel guilty because it seems I'm pushing my love out of my mind. Then I feel better once You touch my mind and I realize the healing process has begun.

I'm not giving up my dream of a perfect life with my love. I've just decided to dream a different dream. A new dream. I've decided to take You up on Your offer Lord. You've given me a different dream and I've decided to live *that* dream! This new dream calls for no vacant spots in my heart. I used to say, "Lord, You made four chambers in my heart, so why is one empty?" You have one, I have one, and my love has one, but I couldn't figure out why one was empty. Well, I finally figured it out Lord and now I know. One's a reservoir. It's around for times like this. A chamber for You, a chamber for me, a chamber for my love in heaven, and a chamber for my second love to be. Now all chambers will be filled. GOD, truly You are a mastermind. You've prepared for the better times ahead. For that Lord, I love You. You've made my heart big enough so I can truly love again.

Lord, thank You. Thank You for being You. Thank You for never leaving my side. Thank You for giving me strength when I was weary. Thank You for carrying me when I couldn't carry myself. Lord, I thank You. In Jesus name I pray – Amen.

Widowhood

GOD the Spouse

[22] *"Ye shall not afflict any widow, or fatherless child.* [23] *If thou afflict them in any wise, and they cry at all unto me, I will surely hear their cry;* [24] *And my wrath shall wax hot, and I will kill you with the sword; and your wives shall be widows, and your children fatherless." ~ Exodus 22:22-24*

[25] *"The LORD will destroy the house of the proud: but he will establish the border of the widow." ~ Proverbs 15:25*

Epistle No. 50
Dear GOD,

I cry myself to sleep each night. I have no one to tuck me in. Why did I have to be the one left alone in this world? Why do I have to fend for myself? Some days I see the light and I enjoy the sunshine. Even now the sun shines, but it always seems like rain on a cloudy day. I try being positive and hopeful, but it's not easy when you have no one to turn to. No one wants me. They all think something is wrong with me. No matter how nice I am, how much I brush my hair and put on my best clothes, they still look at me as a reject. GOD, I don't know what else to do. I have no one to talk to. Everyone in here is in a bad frame of mind. All they talk about are negative things. When I try to be positive and tell them that one day we will all find a home, they all laugh at me and say, "Wishful thinking." They tell me to just pack it up and learn to accept the fact that we *are* the bastards of the earth! Vagabonds, they call us. They tell me not to worry because I do have a family – them! They say we belong to a family of nomads and that nomads are who we are. As long as we stay together, we'll be fine, they say. GOD, that sounds fine and dandy, but I know that's not a real family. That's not the way You intended things to be. I'm supposed to have a father. I'm supposed to have a mother. I'm even supposed to have siblings if this is what You want.

I don't wanna be a reject. I don't want to be a statistic. I don't want to be a vagabond. I'm not a vagabond! I've heard people say kids like me have a grim outlook. They say we're less likely to excel in school, more likely to become delinquents, use drugs, have all sorts of emotional and behavioral issues, become teenage parents out of wedlock and the list goes on. There seems to be so much negativity associated with people like me, so I have to ask You, why me? Why am I here? Why would You leave me or even cause me to be in a situation like this? Do I even have a fighting chance? Is there any hope? I used to ask myself those questions repeatedly until one day You showed me something different. You showed me a different kind of talk. Not different in the sense they spoke of something else, but different in that, for once, they spoke positively. This gave me hope. There's proof that children who have lost their parents tend to have greater career success and overall satisfaction. I'm smart! See, I can even use big words just like the adults. So, GOD, maybe there is hope for me after all. With people like Ella Fitzgerald, Bach, Louis Armstrong, Aristotle, Malcolm X, Mandela, and even one of my favorite authors – Edgar Allan Poe to shadow, my hope has been restored. Yes Lord, my hope has been restored. One day, I too will be the next great orphan.

Orphan

GOD the Parent

[8] "When thou saidst, Seek ye my face; my heart said unto thee, Thy face, LORD, will I seek. [9] Hide not thy face far from me; put not thy servant away in anger: thou hast been my help; leave me not, neither forsake me, O God of my salvation. [10] When my father and my mother forsake me, then the LORD will take me up." ~ Psalm 27:8-10

[11] "Leave thy fatherless children, I will preserve them alive; and let thy widows trust in me." ~ Jeremiah 49:11

Epistle No. 51

Dear GOD,

I never thought I would see my life flash before my eyes. I've always heard stories of people having near-death experiences and witnessing their life flash before their very eyes. I just never thought that would happen to me. I guess I was a little selfish in my thinking because for sure, there's one thing no one can escape, and that is death. So why'd I think I wouldn't experience such a thing? I guess I just never thought about it that hard. Maybe I took things too lightly, You know – having that, "Nonchalant" attitude. Either way Lord, You made me realize, it doesn't take a near-death encounter before someone can become witness to all the pages in *their* book of life.

I could sit and say, "Why me," but that's not going to make things any better. That's a selfish thought. For sure, that will just set me up for failure. Wallowing in the unknown is never a good idea. Well, I suppose I can speak like this now, not because I'm a tough guy, but because I've spent enough time in despair. I mean why not me? Me asking why me, is like me saying, why didn't this happen to someone else.

Somehow Lord, even as stubborn as I am, You managed to work Your way into my heart. You gave me the strength to move on. Once I got past my anger toward You Lord, things seemed to get better. It all hit me *so* suddenly when I realized I'm not on this journey alone. I know You're always there for me. Thank You Lord. I won't say that I don't have days of melancholy and frustration because I do, but then again who doesn't? Sick or not sick, no one gets a pass on that!

It's funny how I used to say I just want to go suddenly. You know, without any warning. I used to feel that way until I got my recent diagnosis. I know most people feel the same and that's probably because they don't realize the benefit of leaving the other way.

I've had plenty of time to think. As a matter of fact, it seems that's all I do nowadays. It's worked on my behalf. Now I take time to notice everything in my life, in this world. Everything has become heightened. The roses, which I never noticed before, seem to let off a more fragrant smell. The sun, when it's shinning, seems to shine brighter. The rain seems to be more soothing, while days of overcast become days of tranquility rather than days of gloom. Even with all that Lord, the best change I've noticed is my attitude toward You. I'm no longer ungrateful. I've learned to appreciate *every* single thing You offer. I no longer take things or life, or You for granted. I'm happy You've given me time. Time is of the essence. Now I have time to allow Jesus to be the Lord and Savior of my life. Now I have time to secure my eternal salvation. I have time to repent for my sins. I have time to repair all broken relationships. I have time to forgive those who've hurt me. I have time to grow stronger in my faith. I have time to help give others hope. And most of all Lord, I have time to love as I've never loved before.

Terminal Illness

GOD the Therapist

[7] "And lest I should be exalted above measure through the abundance of the revelations, there was given to me a thorn in the flesh, the messenger of Satan to buffet me, lest I should be exalted above measure. [8] For this thing I besought the Lord thrice, that it might depart from me. [9] And he said unto me, My grace is sufficient for thee: for my strength is made perfect in weakness. Most gladly therefore will I rather glory in my infirmities, that the power of Christ may rest upon me." ~ 2 Corinthians 12:7-9

Epistle No. 52

Dear GOD,

I'm so **tired** right now. Although I could sit here and whine about it, I won't. You've given me life! I don't want to come across as **ungrateful** because I know this will only make You sad. Father, please forgive me for being such a **user**. I'll call it what it is. I know sometimes I barely give You the time of day and still, You always provide for me. No matter how much I've **used** You Lord, You have *always* remained faithful.

I recall several times when I came to You, **fearful** of something I had done, **venting** my fears, and You never once avoided me. You were always a kind listener. It was constant kindness that has caused me to put things into a **proper perspective**. It was easier to accept, once I realized You're the **architect** of my life.

GOD, thank You for making my mind alert and my heart receptive. That's the reason I know You exist. I will never denounce You as long as I live! I will never become an **atheist** and as long as I live, I'll never identify with **agnosticism**! I know You exist, there's no question about that in my mind. You're a merciful GOD and a GOD who answers prayers. For that, I am **thankful**.

Father, please forgive me when I am **late** with giving You the praise. My intentions are good, but I do get sidetracked. Thank You for understanding me. Lord You know I can be totally **clueless** at times. That's why Lord You *are* the **Omniscient**. I am just so **grateful** You're the Savior. That's a fact I keep in close **remembrance**. I pray this prayer delights You.

I try not to become **self-absorbed** when life throws me through a loop. I've gotten better with casting my cares upon You Father because I'm constantly reminded of Your Supremacy. You *are* truly, *the* **Alpha and *the* Omega**. No matter how much I am **abused** by society, You are *always* there as my biggest supporter.

Father GOD, I am so thankful to You that You've never allowed me to become an **addict** of any kind. You know better than anyone, that this life is brutal and if one allows it, it will push them to the brink of insanity. Thank You for being the **healer** of *all* my wounds.

Forgive me Father, for years of selfish acts. Through seeking You and allowing You to be my **advisor**, I have learned to perform selfless acts. Lord, for that, I thank You. I thank You Lord for keeping me from being a statistic when I was in danger of being **sexually assaulted**. Although You spared me Father, the trauma of the moment marinated in my mind leaving me **restless** and **afraid**. But once again, You stepped in and took on the role of a counselor to see me through it all. I didn't even know how to pray and my approach to You was "**layman**" style, but I found You were **pleased** with my prayers. I came to You as a **child,** and You were **touched**. That was the only way I knew how since I was **just saved**. In my heart, I could feel You rejoicing as You took me from **neonate** to adulthood as only You, the **Omnipotent**, could've done.

Father, thank You for being **sympathetic** during the time I contemplated becoming **anorexic**. I didn't know what else to do because I didn't have any food and I was already famished. Times were so hard that I dreaded becoming **homeless**, but even during that time You watched over me. You are my **guiding light**. That period of my life I thought was a setback, but you were gracious enough to show me that it is a **conquered disability**. You made me realize how **blessed** I am to have a **choreographer** like You on my side. For that Lord, I thank You. I often **wondered** why aren't You here with me Lord when you made it clear You are here, there, and everywhere? You are *the* **Omnipresent**.

GOD, I know You are the **sustainer of life**, and I pray You will bless me to live long enough to be called, "**The Elderly**." You are the chief, You are the **boss**. You are **Sovereign**!

I thank You Lord that I never had to live a life as a **refugee**. Being a refugee may be worse than suffering from **chronic pain**. I pray, knowing I can receive healing, for GOD, You are the reliever of *all* distress. Whenever I pray, I become hopeful. I literally begin to witness a sense of peace come over me.

Thank You, Father, for being a true friend. You love me whether I'm fat or skinny, mean or nice, or even when I'm being a damsel in distress in disguise. Lord, You are Lord of my life. Even with that, I don't think I'll ever get it so right as to be an **upstanding** heavy-laden bishop. Their burden is quite heavy, and I am just so thankful You've called others to hold that post. Can You just imagine Lord how I would become such a **glutton** if I held that post? I would eagerly accept all those lovely dinner invitations. I know You're a mind changer Father, but I don't know, You'd be working overtime trying to change my mind from food! Even being a **pastor**, Father, the same thing would apply. I know You're not pleased with me acting like a **teenager**, but Lord that's just an area where I really fall short.

Lord, I can't help but be **humble** as I see the ways You have dealt with me and others. You're always kind, caring, and gentle when You deal with us. You are the **perfect parent**. How gracious You've been to so many. I thank You for stepping in for all those **single parents** acting as the head of the house for every family, friends, and brothers and sisters in Christ. Hum, Lord, since we're on the subject of *single* . . . Lord You know I'm still single. I'm not sweating it though because I know You're the perfect matchmaker. So until You decide to bless me with my perfect someone, I will continue to settle for blissful thoughts of becoming a **newlywed**. I will have blissful thoughts of becoming a parent. I will have blissful thoughts of living in the overflow. I know You are the master multiplier and You *will* bless me with beautiful and healthy, GOD blessed, angel kissed babies.

Forgive me Lord, whenever I act like an **unbeliever**; doubting those things You've promised me. Even when I get impatient and doubt creeps into my mind, You always remain **patient** with me. GOD, for that, I thank You. Lord, You are so kind, always thinking of Your children first. You even sent Your only begotten Son, my Lord, and Savior Jesus Christ of Nazareth. You sent Him to die on the cross so that whosoever will, may have eternal salvation with You. For that Lord, I love You.

Thank You Father for always making me feel as if I belong. So many times, this crazy world makes me feel like an **alien** – as if I'm dead to the world. Nevertheless, You *are* the **way maker**. You sure do know how to make me feel alive. You keep me from **dying**, even when my soul gets weak. I am so open now to be the receiver of *all* the good things You have in store for me. One thing I know is, You'll send me a wonderful partner soon because You know how difficult single life can be. Hey, listen Lord, I'm not a **racist**. I'm willing and ready to accept whoever You send my way, but I do have a tiny request. Lord, please make sure You're the pruner of this man. Make sure You get rid of any rough edges he and I have before You mold us together. No **cheaters** allowed either Lord because I don't know if I'm that strong to forgive and forget. I know You're the seer of *all* things, so I'm confident You'll make sure all is well before delivering my Mr. Right. An **upstanding** man, an extraordinary man, a Mr. Debonair who blesses all good and pure things, will do just fine.

Father GOD, as I pray for my perfect mate, I must take a moment to pray for the widows of the world. I couldn't imagine having to live life after the death of a spouse. Console and keep them Lord because they need You more than ever. They need Your love.

Lord I pray for the **orphans** as well, – the children of **widows**, the children who've lost both parents, and the children whose parents are lost. They need Your comfort and love Lord. You know better than anyone how fragile and innocent most of them are. Father, watch over them, protect and guide them and give them the love that only You can give.

Forgive us Father for the times we cause our minds to succumb to a terrible **terminal illness**. You know Father, the **illness** of proud looks, lying, murder, devising wicked plans, giving in to evil, bearing false witness, and for being troublemakers. GOD, for these sins I repent. Lord, I ask for mercy and forgiveness for my friends who are guilty of such sins.

Thank You Lord for being a constant pillar of strength. You *are* the **greatest therapist**!

GOD, have I told You I am so very thankful to have You in my corner? Without You, I am, and I would be nothing! Without You, I would be so lost and so weary. Father, I thank You for giving me rest on days like today when clearly, I'm **exhausted**. I love You, I thank You, I praise You, I worship You, I honor and I *absolutely* adore You. Oh Lord, I thank You Father for being the Supreme You. I thank You Father for being the *Great* **I Am**. I thank You Father for being You. In Jesus Christ of Nazareth's holy and precious name I pray – Amen.

Thankful Sophie

GOD the Great I Am

[9] "After this manner therefore pray ye: Our Father which art in heaven, Hallowed be thy name. [10] Thy kingdom come, Thy will be done in earth, as it is in heaven. [11] Give us this day our daily bread. [12] And forgive us our debts, as we forgive our debtors. [13] And lead us not into temptation, but deliver us from evil: For thine is the kingdom, and the power, and the glory, forever. Amen." ~ Matthew 6:9-13

Epistle No. 53

Dear GOD,

Good night.

Exhausted

GOD of Rest

[28] *"Come unto me, all ye that labour and are heavy laden, and I will give you rest. [29] Take my yoke upon you, and learn of me; for I am meek and lowly in heart: and ye shall find rest unto your souls. [30] For my yoke is easy, and my burden is light." ~ Matthew 11:28-30*

The prayers of men are ended.

Afterword

One's prayer must be sincere unto the LORD. In the chapter titled Prayer and Praying of my book, *Christianity 101: The ABC's and 123's of The Faith*, I emphasize that prayer and praying should not be made into a ritual ("an act or series of acts regularly repeated in a set precise manner; according to *religious law*"). Prayer should never be nor become ritualistic. If you are a Christian, I pray you know we are no longer under the Law. All Christians have been *saved by the grace* of GOD by way of Jesus Christ of Nazareth! Amen!

Again, I reiterate, your prayer life in no way, shape, or form should ever become ritualistic. I cannot stress this point enough. Having said that, please know that kneeling, head coverings, lighting a candle, and the like during your prayer time *is not* forbidden. However, none of those 3 actions are neither required or necessary. GOD *hears you* all day long regardless of your setup.

Brethren, it behooves you to develop the habit of praying throughout the day. Talk to GOD. Talk to the Father while you exercise, clean, walk, run, lounge, and of course during whatever time you designate to pray.

Praying while in the shower may seem vile to some, however, know there are truly no off-limits circumstances or environments for prayer and praying. If you've been taught as such or someone has tried to make you feel bad for not ascribing to any of the aforementioned scenarios, you have full permission to dismiss their comments regarding the matter!

If you are new to Christianity and you haven't read my book, *Christianity 101: The ABC's and 123's of The Faith*, I highly recommend you do so. In that book, I provide the basics of the Christian faith in an easy-to-read fashion. Just a quick note, most of my books, if not all, will follow the same easy to read style.

Consider the following excerpt from Chapter 3 titled Prayer and Praying from the book *Christianity 101* which sums up the general thinking one should have surrounding prayer and praying.

"In the book of Matthew 6:9-13, we read of Jesus Christ of Nazareth providing His disciples with the following model prayer when they asked Him how to pray.

The Model Prayer

[9]"...Our Father which art in heaven,
Hallowed be thy name.
[10] Thy kingdom come,
Thy will be done in earth, as it is in heaven.
[11] Give us this day our daily bread.
[12] And forgive us our debts,
as we forgive our debtors.
[13] And lead us not into temptation,
but deliver us from evil one:
For thine is the kingdom, and the power, and the glory
forever. Amen.

In Matthew-6:5-8 Jesus outlines the dos and don'ts of prayer. Don't pray to be seen nor pray a repetitive prayer. Instead, pray to be heard by the Father and without praying as if the Father doesn't already know your desires and needs. Despite this not being included in the actual Model Prayer, it is just as important to note as they are instructions from the LORD.

The Model Prayer is exactly as the name implies, it's a model. Jesus merely recited the above prayer for the disciples as an illustration of how they ought to pray. He did not say to use vain repetitions, nor did He say this is the *only* way to pray. Jesus didn't instruct kneeling, head covering, candle burning, or any other ritualistic act. I reiterate, when the disciples asked Him how to pray, He gave them the model prayer found in the New Testament. (*Side note: The New Testament is the portion of the Bible that starts with the book of Matthew and goes until the end of the book of Revelation*).

The Bible says to pray without ceasing, give thanks unto GOD, repent (ask for forgiveness of sins) and let your wants and needs be known unto GOD. *16 "Rejoice evermore. 17 Pray without ceasing. 18 In everything give thanks: for this is the will of GOD in Christ Jesus concerning you."* ~ 1 Thessalonians 5:16 -18. *6 "Be careful for nothing, but in everything by prayer and supplication with thanksgiving let your requests be made known unto GOD. And the peace of GOD, which passeth all understanding, shall keep your hearts and minds through Christ Jesus."* ~ <u>Philippians -4:6-7</u>. The Bible also says to ask and so we shall receive. *7 "Ask, and it shall be given you; seek, and ye shall find; knock, and it shall be opened unto you:..."* ~ <u>Matthew 7:7</u>. Those 3 scriptures clearly illustrate the nonspecific nature of prayer. Simply put, prayer is a way of communicating with GOD. Prayer is key to building your relationship with the LORD. Thanking GOD for His provisions and acknowledging His Sovereignty is essential for all believers of growth. One's prayer shouldn't merely consist of asking GOD for things, but instead, the aim should *always* be an attitude of gratitude, the acknowledgment of GOD's sovereignty, and praying for GOD's will to be done in your life. You may be wondering if asking for your heart's desire is wrong, the answer is no. However, solely asking for the desires of your heart, not being thankful, and failing to ask GOD for His *perfect will* to be done in your life *will not* lead you into the full manifestation of a prosperous purpose-filled life. Being thankful (having an attitude of gratitude) and asking GOD for His *perfect will* to be done in your life is indeed the highest form of prayer.

Chapter 22 in the book of Luke shadows Jesus when He was in the garden of Gethsemane. Verse 41- 42 notes Jesus praying to the Father in the following manner: *41 "And he was withdrawn from them about a stone's cast, and kneeled down, and prayed, Saying, Father, if thou be willing, remove this cup from me: nevertheless not my will, but thine, be done."* Again, praying the Father's will be done and thanking Him *is* the highest form of prayer. If Jesus of Nazareth prayed as such, then every believer in Christ ought to pray as such."

The Salvation Prayer

Well, here we are, at the end of our journey together for now. Thank GOD this journey can continue throughout eternity if you make the decision today to give your life to Jesus Christ of Nazareth. Beloved, the only way to spend eternity with GOD Almighty is to give your life to Jesus Christ, confess with your mouth and believe in your heart that Jesus is LORD and Savior. This *is* the most important decision you will ever make in your life! Remember, the only way to the Father is through the Son, His Son, Jesus Christ of Nazareth. If you wish to step into a magnificently beautiful relationship with the Father and journey with Abba, the One who matters above all, please say the following prayer aloud and mean it from your heart:

Father GOD I believe I will be saved by accepting and professing Jesus Christ of Nazareth as my personal LORD and Savior because You've said in Your Word that we are

saved by grace through faith which is a gift from You Father. Your Word says You so loved the world that You gave Your only begotten Son to die for our sins so that whoever believes in Him shall not perish, but have everlasting life. Father GOD, I confess I am a sinner and I am asking for Your forgiveness of all my sins. Father please wash me, cleanse me and make me whole again. Help me to turn from my wicked and sinful ways and to walk righteously in Your sight. So Father GOD as there is nothing I can do to earn salvation except accepting Your Son as my LORD and Savior, I believe and confess right now that Jesus Christ of Nazareth is my LORD and Savior, the Savior of the world, Your only begotten Son who died on the cross for me, bearing all my sins and rose again on the 3rd day. I believe with all my heart Jesus Christ of Nazareth, Your Son who was dead but You rose Him from the dead is alive today. Father, it is by faith I receive Your Son as my LORD and Savior. In doing so, I believe I am now saved and will spend eternity in heaven with You Abba Father. I thank You Father for loving me and never leaving me. I will forever be grateful. In the name of Jesus Christ of Nazareth, I pray, Amen.

Now that you've said the prayer, know that **to be saved**, it's as simple as confessing what the Word of GOD says in Romans 10:9, *"If thou shalt confess with thy mouth the LORD Jesus and believe in your heart that GOD has raised Him from the dead, thou shalt be saved."*

A Blessing from the LORD

22 "And the Lord spake unto Moses, saying,

23 Speak unto Aaron and unto his sons, saying, On this wise ye shall bless the children of Israel, saying unto them,

24 The Lord bless thee, and keep thee:

25 The Lord make his face shine upon thee, and be gracious unto thee:

26 The Lord lift up his countenance upon thee, and give thee peace.

27 And they shall put my name upon the children of Israel, and I will bless them."

~ Numbers 6:22-27 ~

171

Endnotes

Afterword

1. *Merriam-Webster.com*, "Ritual," Merriam-Webster Dictionary, 2020. https://www.merriam-webster.com/dictionary/ritual (Accessed June. 12, 2020).

About the Author

Serving as an interim radio co-host, guest minister/speaker at multiple churches, schools, community affairs, and radio programs, Dr. SOPHIA MATTIS' voice has been heard via various venues.

Dr. Mattis is a Jamaican native, devout Christian, physician, motivational speaker, writer, and lecturer residing in Long Island, New York. Holding degrees in Medicine, Health Services Administration, and Sociology, Dr. Mattis has proven to be well rounded and passionate about the well-being of mankind. She is focused and determined to heal the minds of GOD's children by way of the Word of GOD. Dr. Mattis' love for GOD nourishes her mission to heal the mind of the destitute by working heavily with disadvantaged youths, the elderly, and the homeless. Through her works, she hopes to usher in the *Light* of GOD into the dark places in the minds of those she encounters. Dr. Sophia Mattis' mission is to win countless souls for Jesus Christ of Nazareth.

Throughout the years, Dr. Mattis has written numerous health and wellness newspaper articles while providing weekly encouraging segments for various online Christian newspapers. Currently, Dr. Mattis has published *Christianity 101: The ABC's and 123's of The Faith* and *Our Father's Pot Daily Journal Plus Affirmations*. She has several Christian books pending publication.

Spearheading events such as: the United Nation's International Day of Peace – (an initiative focusing on combat gang violence within her community), N.A.C.I. – Never Alone Care Initiative – an initiative providing toiletries to the less fortunate), and OFP – Our Father's Pot – (a monthly gathering where women discuss pressing matters), are some of the undertakings she engages. To help combat hunger and homelessness on Long Island, Dr. Mattis helps distribute food both at her local church and soup kitchen. Dr. Mattis is an active *Biometrics Medical Review Board Member* who continuously seeks out volunteering opportunities during her travels, to assist in enhancing dilapidated communities and feeding those who are less fortunate.

Dr. Mattis' love for GOD, His people, evangelism, healing, teaching, and philanthropy, motivates her to minister the Word of GOD worldwide. She attributes her knowledge of the Word to the Holy Spirit's teaching and leading.

Contact the Author

Sophia Mattis, M.D., M.H.S.A

209 Glen Cove Road, Suite 508

Carle Place, NY 11514

Asksophiebella3@gamil.com

www.asksophiebella3.wixsite.com/mysite

Book Information

OTHER BOOKS BY DR. SOPHIA MATTIS

Christianity 101: The ABC's and 123's of The Faith

Our Father's Pot Daily Journal Plus Affirmations

DR. SOPHIA MATTIS' UPCOMING BOOKS

Christianity 101: The ABC's and 123's of The Faith Study Guide

30 Days of Gratitude: Use Your Words to Change Your Life

In the Beginning: Genesis Reviewed

TOL – Thinking Out Loud: A Weekly Meditation

Gratitude

Thank you for your purchase.

Thank you for taking time to read.

Thank you for being a blessing!

Index

J

H

L

I

M

Made in the USA
Middletown, DE
03 July 2021